GIVING UP IS NOT AN OPTION

Memoirs of a Palestinian American

Hani Q. Khoury

with the original book cover illustration by Teresa Abboud

Copyright

Hani Q. Khoury

Giving Up Is Not an Option: Memoirs of a Palestinian American

Text by Hani Q. Khoury © 2021
Coloring of the book cover illustration copyright © 2021 T. Abboud

All rights reserved. No part of this publication may be reproduced, distributed, or transmitted in any form or by any means, or stored in a database or retrieval system without the prior written permission of the publisher.

Hani Q. Khoury
Khoury_hq@mercer.edu

ISBN 979-8-9854303-1-8

Table of Contents

Foreword iv

Introduction & Acknowledgements vi

Chapter One: Palestine — A Childhood with Conflict 1

Chapter Two: My Journey to America 47

Chapter Three: Education Despite Disability 66

Chapter Four: Embracing a Nation and a Family 92

Chapter Five: Mathematics Education and the Future of Democracy

    — A Professional Perspective 107

Chapter Six: Visiting with the Past 118

Chapter Seven: Conclusion 143

References 146

Foreword

What you are about to read is an incredible story from and about a remarkable man. Hani Khoury has been for almost thirty years a treasured member of the faculty of Mercer University. He is a mathematics educator of the first order and a human being of the highest grade. His PhD degree in mathematics education from Syracuse University is abundant testimony to his academic prowess and to the consistently diligent work that characterizes almost everything that Hani touches. He is respected and revered by all who know him, and all who know him are all the better because of it.

I met Hani on April 15, 1994, at the Hampton Inn in Forsyth, Georgia, where we had agreed to meet for an initial interview regarding a teaching position in the mathematics faculty of University College at Mercer. That day was the beginning of almost thirty years of an unparalleled commitment to the education of students in both mathematics and in an even broader development of a deep moral awareness of our mutual societal obligations as responsible citizens.

From my initial encounter with Hani in 1994, I have learned that being confined to a wheelchair does not imply or make necessary a life of helplessness. As best I can recall, I have never seen Hani not in his wheelchair. He drove a van specially equipped for a driver with a severe handicap. He went almost anywhere he desired or was needed, alone or with passengers. Hani is not confined to a life of isolation due to his limitations, and he seems scarcely aware of what his own physical limitations would mean for the rest of us. As you read, you will most likely be amazed at his openness to and his participation in world events that might affect us all, and you may well be almost incredulous as he describes for his readers his journeys back to his homeland on the West Bank of the Jordan River in the Palestinian Territories. The deeper you get into his story, the more impressed you will probably be that physical limitations are not inevitably prohibitive, and as Hani describes for his readers where he has come from and how he has dealt with his challenges, you will most likely admire, if not envy, his ability to make the most out of the least that anyone can even imagine.

In 2013, my wife and I had the privilege of traveling with Hani and a group of Mercer students to Amman, Jordan, where for three weeks those students, under Hani's guidance, conducted a recreational camp for orphaned Jordanian children. At our first gathering with those orphaned children, I sat in amazement as they watched and listened in rapt attention to this handicapped man in a wheelchair who spoke to them in their own native tongue as he began the process of making friends with those young children who may well have been a bit skeptical as to what we were about and why we were there in their midst. I couldn't help but wonder if those young children might have seen in Hani some hopeful sign of what might someday become of them. My own eyes filled with unexpected moisture as I watched those children who perhaps wondered what they might be able someday to do with their own lives.

Hani has included in his book photographs from the time of his own childhood all the way to his most recent days. You may find yourself enthralled as you look carefully at the photographic glimpses of Hani's family and of the myriad of friendships he has made throughout his journeys. I think I can almost guarantee you an occasional smile and even a tear or two as you get visually in touch with who Hani is and where he has come from. Hani is my friend, and if I had no others, I would be grateful for what he has meant to all of us at Mercer and most pointedly what he has meant and what he continues to mean to me.

Duane E. Davis, PhD
Professor Emeritus of Philosophy and Religion
Mercer University
October 30, 2021

Introduction & Acknowledgements

Nearly forty years have passed since I left my native home in the heart of the Middle East for a new home and a new life in a faraway place called America. In the pages that follow, I will tell the story of my departure from that long-disputed land and my journey to a world that has become for me a place of new beginnings and friendships, unforeseen challenges, and personal and professional accomplishments.

The long and difficult road I have traveled has helped make me the person I have become, and what you are about to read are my reflections on what it has been like to go about the task of healing the physical and emotional scars of my early years and of finding new reasons for hope and new avenues of service in a life and in a profession that both sustain and give purpose to my chosen career in the classroom.

The first eighteen years of my life stand as a testimony to the struggles of a wounded spirit in a wounded land. I call that land Palestine; others call it Israel—and oh, how many painful memories I have of that place so many others call the "Holy Land." The thirty-eight years since my arrival in America stand as a testimony to how I have determined to live to the fullest of my abilities and defeat the many typical and prejudicial perceptions of people with disabilities found in an even open and democratic society.

Many of my early memories are grounded in a childhood that was tormented by unusually difficult challenges. Other and later memories are grounded in my subsequent journey to adulthood and independence. In the upcoming story I will do my best to depict the past truthfully and openly. Occasionally, I will have to rely on research to support my personal narrative, but I have nothing to fear from controversy. On the contrary, I welcome it if based on respectful differences of opinion and intellectual honesty.

I was born in Nablus, Palestine in 1965 with a rare and progressive physical disorder known as Spinal Muscular Atrophy, a neuromuscular disease that sentenced me to an electric wheelchair at the age of 18. With an increasing weakness and loss of muscle mass, I am writing this autobiography with the assistance of voice-activated computer software. How fortunate I am to be living in the age of assistive technologies!

I grew up in a Christian family that stood at the crossroads of a blended set of Christian and Muslim beliefs, Samaritan and Jewish cultural and religious influences, and secular values. Growing up with various traditions helped me throughout my life develop multiple and global perspectives on a spectrum of questions and challenges. Although my last name, Khoury, means "priest" in the Arabic language, my life at home and in the community was governed mostly by Arab and Islamic values and traditions. Today, I am a secularist who stands firmly against all forms of fundamentalism and intolerant views, religious or otherwise.

Disability was not my only challenge as a child. On June 5th, 1967, two years after my birth, the Six-Day War between Israel and the surrounding Arab states began. The war lasted for only six days, ending with a shocking Israeli victory. Nablus, my birthplace, one of the largest cities in the West Bank, came under the rule of the Israeli military occupation. I had no idea as a child how destructive a military occupation can be on the lives of both the occupied and the occupiers.

In 1973, the Yom Kippur War, also known as the Ramadan or October War, fought between Israel and the Arab states, introduced another round of military confrontation. At the age of 8, I began to realize that my life was being filled with doubts and questions. As a young boy, I was being shattered by the misfortunes of war and injustice, seemingly endless questions concerning my disability, the Israeli occupation, and my own social identity as a Palestinian, all of which haunted me day and night. I was a child with a Christian background living in a predominantly Muslim society, and my confusion regarding both my personal and social identity was palpable.

I didn't really know who I was, and I was bewildered by the prospects and challenges that confronted me daily.

Throughout my childhood years, and then as a young adult, questions concerning freedom, independence, body image, personhood, and the purpose and meaning of life confronted me daily. Living among Muslims, Christians, Samaritans, believers in God and atheists, I felt a desperate need to find my own truth, but I didn't know where to look for answers. There were simply too many gods and all of them seemed different. In the end, I felt left with no alternative but to leave my homeland in search of another. America, it turned out, was to be my destination.

Accompanied by my parents, I began my journey to freedom on August 12, 1983, when our plane from Amman, Jordan landed at JFK International Airport in New York City. My new life began that day in a country that was and remains known for its freedoms and the rule of law. In this new world of mine and with the help of new and advanced technologies, I was able to leave the past for a new and promising future. In my newly adopted country, I was able to obtain my higher education, form a family, gain employment, and become a productive member of society, just like anyone else. In this "greatest country of all" that we call America, I have met many wonderful people from different faiths and backgrounds. Their unparalleled humanity and support have made it possible for me to live out the truth that "when and where there is a will, there is a way."

In the following chapters, I will narrate some of the highlights of both the complexities of my life and the events that have nurtured it. My story as a person with a physical disability is, like many other stories, filled with challenges, setbacks, hopes, and dreams. The juxtaposition of two very different cultural settings — Israeli-occupied Palestine in the heart of the Middle East and the United States of America — will, I hope, provide the reader with a deeper understanding of the meaning and implications of liberty and self-determination, both individually and collectively.

Introduction & Acknowledgements   ix

One of the greatest fortunes in life is to have good friends and family members who are willing to listen to you and encourage and support you throughout your ventures. I can gratefully say that I was fortunate in this regard.

I would like to express my special thanks of gratitude for several friends and colleagues who encouraged me to begin my work, persevere with it, and finally to publish it. I am grateful to my very dear friend and colleague Duane E. Davis, Professor Emeritus at Mercer University. I would not have been able to get through my professional journey at Mercer and publish this book without the continued support and encouragement of Duane.

I am also grateful to my dear friend Patrick A. Gibby for his help, guidance, and computer expertise. Patrick's knowledge and assistance turned the pages of this book into a reality.

I am indebted to my book readers at Mercer University: Professors Hollis Phelps and Jared Champion for their insightful remarks and suggestions. I am also thankful to Ms. Teresa Abboud, an Atlanta-based artist and illustrator, for her creative design of the book cover.

I dedicate my narrative to all those who have made and continue to make a difference in my life. A special dedication goes out to my wife, my parents, and my children who have stood beside me through the years.

I am also grateful to my teachers in Palestine and the US, as well as mentors and colleagues at Syracuse University and Mercer University. From the heart of Palestine to the hearts of New York and Georgia, a special dedication goes out to all seekers and makers of peace throughout this troubled world — peace, not as the absence of war, but as the collective commitment to the protection and prosperity of every human life. A special call for peace with justice goes out to all people, especially in Palestine, for the sake of Israelis and Palestinians alike. A loud call for peace with justice goes out to Israel and to the Israeli people to end their occupation of Palestine. A cry for forgiveness goes out to the Palestinian people for enduring pain and suffering under Israeli military occupation. It is my hope that wisdom will prevail over prolonged sufferings of all inhabitants of the Middle East.

Today, I stand as a firm believer in the immense contributions of education — including mathematics education — to humanity. I believe that it is through education that the world stands a chance to reform and heal itself. Moving forward in 'our' world requires that all of us confront our own fears with reason, knowledge, and thoughtfulness. It is through education that we liberate ourselves and one another.

Teaching is an integral part of education. It is a vocation and it's about nurturing and enriching the lives of others. I am a passionate teacher because I see myself as a byproduct of the caring and encouragement I have received from countless others. This includes my parents and other family members, K-12 teachers, university professors, mentors, friends, and colleagues. To all of them I must say "Thank You".

A few final words to all who seek knowledge, especially to my students: The world needs you now more than ever! I strongly encourage you to learn and value mathematics as a structure for critical thinking and reflection. I'm asking you to appreciate mathematics for its innermost beauty: its dynamics and tools that help us understand constructive change in life as a derivative of pondering, and of freedom as a derivative of democratic thinking. As Barry Mazur of Harvard University once said: "... Mathematics is one of humanities' long continuing conversations with itself."

Chapter One: Palestine — A Childhood with Conflict

Introduction

In this chapter, I will describe what it was like to be born with a disability and to live as a Palestinian under the Israeli military occupation. I will present the cultural context in which disability and harsh political reality coexisted. I will concentrate on the reality I was facing as a child and as a young adult which led me to leave everything and almost everyone else behind and look forward to a meaningful life elsewhere.

Images from the past still haunt me as I have clear memories of a time and place in which I was deprived of basic freedoms, political as well as physical. The political climate, together with my being born with a physical disability, made uncertainty of any meaningful future an integral part of my everyday life for eighteen years. Fear, the worst enemy of all and my constant daily foe, forced me to confront my limitations with courage and determination simply to survive from day to day.

Born Without Freedoms

I was born the youngest of four children—two boys and two girls. I am the grandson of a Greek Orthodox priest and the son of an assistant bank manager who lost his job in 1967 as an immediate outcome of the Six-Day War between Israel, on the one hand, and Egypt, Syria, and Jordan on the other. I am the son of a mother who was born in Jaffa near Tel Aviv in 1929 during the British mandate of Palestine. After the First World War, Palestine came under British rule after the defeat of the Ottoman Empire. Prior to marriage, my mother was a teacher in a German missionary school called Talitha Qumi, outside of Bethlehem in a little town called Beit Jala, a few miles south of Jerusalem.

Teaching staff at Talitha Qumi boarding school for girls, Beit Jala, Palestine - circa 1945; mother is seated at the lower-right

Nablus, my birthplace, is one of the largest cities in what is known as the West Bank, a landlocked territory west of the Jordan River sharing boundaries with Israel to the west and Jordan to the east. I remember next to nothing about the war; I was only two years old when it began.

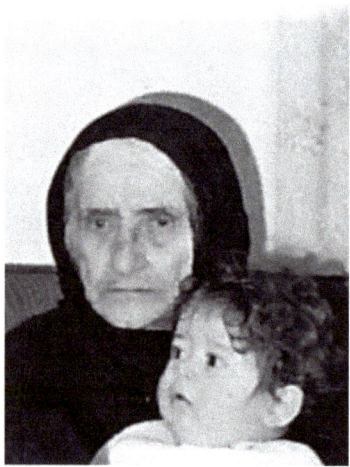

In the arms of my blind paternal grandmother Haniyya (left) My mother Laurice and me (right)

Chapter One: Palestine — A Childhood with Conflict

From birth, I suffered from a rare disease that could not be accurately diagnosed in any major hospital in the Middle East. Neither at Hadassah Hospital, a major Israeli hospital in Jerusalem, nor at the medical center of the American University of Beirut in Lebanon could an exact diagnosis be determined. My parents were informed by doctors that I had a form of muscular dystrophy, an umbrella label for nearly forty muscular and neuromuscular diseases. It was only in 1983 at the University Hospital of Syracuse University in New York that Dr. Carl Crosley, a neurologist and researcher in neuromuscular diseases, diagnosed my medical condition as Spinal Muscular Atrophy (SMA).[1]

As a person living with SMA, I experienced a gradual and progressive physical weakness, and I could only wonder, WHY ME? I had probably asked this question every time I had fallen and had difficulty getting back up to a standing position, or whenever I couldn't do a physical activity requiring any considerable amount of strength. It was evident at the very young age of three or four years that something was wrong with my body. Up to the age of eighteen, I walked very slowly and cautiously, as I limped from one side to the other. Having SMA was a debilitating hardship that I feared would be a life sentence.

Another misfortune was to live and grow up under one of the most brutal military occupations in the world. I found myself caught between two groups of people making the same claim to the land that hugged me every time I fell to the ground. The Israelis called it the "Promised Land," but for Palestinians it was the "Homeland." My parents realized that the conflict between the two sides could extend for years, even decades, and that was indeed the case. The two opposing claims would be too difficult to reconcile without colossal wisdom and good will,

---

[1] Spinal muscular atrophy (SMA) is a genetic disease affecting the central nervous system, peripheral nervous system, and voluntary muscle movement (skeletal muscle). Most of the nerve cells that control muscles are located in the spinal cord, which accounts for the word spinal in the name of the disease. SMA is muscular because its primary effect is on muscles, which don't receive signals from these nerve cells. Atrophy is the medical term for getting smaller, which is what generally happens to muscles when they're not stimulated by nerve cells. (from mda.org)

neither of which saw the light of day. The brutality of the Israeli occupation reached people and things alike, both living and dead.

My family's second rental house in Nablus, my first, was owned by the Alkukhun family, a kind Muslim family. I lived in that house during my first four years. My family then moved to another house on the western edge of the city known as Rafidya. That house was within walking distance from what was going to be my first school, *Beit Al-Tifel*, or *The Child's Home*. I stayed there for only one year, as a first grader, before I transferred to a full-fledged elementary school.

My first house (first floor)

Entering Kindergarten

Entrance to Beit Al-Tifel School (K-1st grade)

When Israel occupied the West Bank, my father went into a severe depression after the bank he had worked for was shut down by the Israeli authorities. Israel wanted to establish full control and dominance over

Chapter One: Palestine — A Childhood with Conflict

Palestinian lives in the newly occupied territories and began to rule with an iron fist in a relentless effort to drive even more Palestinians out of their homeland.

My father had worked as a branch manager of the *Al-Ahli Bank*, headquartered in Amman, Jordan on the eastern side of the Jordan River. Fortunately, the bank continued to pay him a reduced salary even though the branch at which he had worked was no longer in business. My father's subsequent availability at home complemented my mother's main responsibility of caring for me, the youngest of the four children.

Every morning, my mother would wake me up, help me dress, feed me a light breakfast, and then walk me to school. On the way to school, on several occasions, I remember falling to the ground. Sometimes I would ask my mother to stop walking, which would allow me some time to relax and catch my breath. Shortly thereafter I would arrive at school and make my way to my classroom.

Classes began around 8:30 a.m., and at about 10:30 a.m. we were allowed to go to the playground for a 30-minute break. One major obstacle I had to confront was the number of steps I had to descend going down to the playground and then climbing back up to the classroom. Occasionally, I gave up going down to the playground and instead I invited some of my friends to stay with me nearby or inside the classroom during break. Abruptly, my mother would appear in front of me at around 10:45 a.m. to bring me a glass of warm milk blended with the yolk of a poached egg. My mother was hoping that with appropriate nutrition, I would be able to claim a tiny victory over my physical weakness!

I always had difficulty with stairs, and I had to rely on someone else's physical assistance even to walk on level ground, and especially to climb stairs. I had to hold a friend's shoulder to avoid falling. Whenever I did fall, I had to deal with the embarrassment of getting back up.

That period was unforgiving. Many of my schoolmates would make fun of the way I walked, while others tried to comfort me by saying to those who mocked me, "Don't make fun of him; this is the way God (Allah or Al-Rubb) has created him." Allah or Al-Rubb are common Arabic words among Christians and Muslims alike. In the Quran, and during worship ceremonies, God is referred to by the word "Al-Rubb" or "Al-Ilah." These are Arabic alternatives for the word "Allah." "Al-Ilah" is a derivative of 'Allah" emphasizing the singularity of the creator, while "Al-Rubb" emphasizes the head of creation.

An official language of the United Nations and a semitic language that enjoys a very rich, varied and vast literary heritage dating back to the pre-Islamic era, classical Arabic derived from Aramaic, much like its sister languages Hebrew and Amharic, and is used throughout the Arab world from Morocco in the West to Bahrain in the East (about 400 million people), both as the language of instruction, in Arabic broadcast media, in all written publications, government business and the legal system, as well as the liturgical language for about a billion and a half Muslims around the world. The vernacular version of classical Arabic (or Modern standard Arabic) known as 'Aamiyya or Lahja or Darija depending on the region, is spoken in the street by everyone, differs at varying degrees form a region to another, is not written nor is it taught in schools like Modern Standard Arabic, and is naturally acquired as the mother tongue. (Wesleyan University)

Nablus: My Birth City

Nablus, the city of my birth, with a population of nearly 130,000, is engraved in my mind and soul. There is not one day that goes by without a memory of that ancient and beautiful city. Nablus lies in the northern West Bank of the Jordan River, roughly thirty miles north of Jerusalem. Located between Mount Ebal and Mount Gerizim, Nablus is the capital of the Nablus District and is a Palestinian commercial and cultural center.

Chapter One: Palestine — A Childhood with Conflict

A view of Mount Gerizim, October 2018

The sunset over Nablus, October 2018

A view of Mount Ebal.
Source: https://www.dooz.ps/p/88794

[Nablus] was founded in 72 CE/AD by the Roman Emperor Vespasian as *Flavia Neapolis* and has been ruled by many empires over its 2000-year history. In the 5th and 6th centuries, conflict erupted and persisted between the city's Christian and Samaritan inhabitants, climaxing in Samaritan revolts against Byzantine rule, which drastically reduced the Samaritan population. In 636 CE, Neapolis, along with most of Palestine, came under the rule of the Islamic Arab Caliphate of Umar ibn al-Khattab, and the city's name was changed to the Arabic *Nablus*. In 1099, Christian Crusaders took control of the city for almost a century, leaving its Muslim, Christian, and Samaritan population relatively undisturbed. In 1187, the Ayyubid forces of Saladin [a Muslim Sultan of Egypt and Syria] took control of the interior of Palestine [after defeating a massive army of Crusaders in the Battle of Hattin]. [As an outcome], Islamic rule was reestablished and continued under the Mamluk and Ottoman empires.

In 1517, Nablus was incorporated into the Ottoman empire and was designated capital of the district of *Jabal Nablus* (Mount Nablus). By 1841, Nablus prospered as a center of trade. In 1922, following the loss of the city to British forces during World War I, Nablus was incorporated into the British Mandate of Palestine and was designated to form part of the Arab state of Palestine under the 1947 UN partition plan. During the 1948 Arab Israeli War, Nablus was captured and occupied by Transjordan, which later unilaterally annexed it until its occupation by Israel during the 1967 Six-Day War.

Today, Nablus is predominantly Muslim with small Christian and Samaritan minorities which account for 1.2% of the total population of about 131,000, excluding the surrounding refugee camps. Since 1995, the city has been governed by the Palestinian National Authority. In the Old City there are numerous significant archaeological sites from the 1st to the 15th centuries. The city is known for its *Knafeh*, a popular

Chapter One: Palestine — A Childhood with Conflict

dessert throughout the Middle East, and for its olive-oil soap industry. (Nablus 2020)

Homemade Knafeh made from shredded dough, sweet cheese, refined butter, and honey/sugar syrup

Al-Nasr Mosque, 1187 AD — Old City of Nablus

It was in Nablus, with its diversity and long history, that I grew up. During that time, the Israeli military was in full control. Palestinians living in the West Bank were granted Israeli ID cards. As the occupation remained over the years, so did the apartheid-like policies as they continued to intensify (Carter, 2006).

Palestinian cars had blue license plates while Israeli cars had yellow plates. Palestinians had to obtain permits from the Israeli authorities to travel abroad. Palestinians in East Jerusalem could not build new homes without permits, which were seldom granted. Severe policies related to security, housing, schools, and sanitation services were also implemented to the detriment of Palestinian residents in East Jerusalem. The goal was to obstruct Palestinian population growth in the city (Cheshin, Hutman & Melamed, 2002). New laws were implemented regarding land ownership by those who were absent from their lands. Such laws were known as Absentee Laws that allowed the Israeli government to confiscate land and property from absent owners. "Absent" here refers to those who owned property but resided outside of the occupied territories. Certain roads and highways within the occupied areas were built for the sole use of Israeli settlers. Nowadays, the biggest symbol of apartheid-like conditions is a wall separating Palestinians from other Palestinians and from Israelis. Like the Berlin wall, it is meant to separate people based on national identity.

My paternal grandfather was an ordained priest in the Greek Orthodox Church. He lived in a village near Nablus called *Nisf Jubeil*, and he died four years before I was born. His name was Nicola (Arabic for Nicolas). The village is about 10 miles northwest of Nablus near the historic village and archaeological Roman site of Sebastia. It's believed that Sebastia is the burial site of St. John the Baptist. The Archdiocese of Sebastia is named after this historic village, and it is part of the Greek Orthodox Patriarchate of Jerusalem. Archbishop Hanna Atalla, a Palestinian, had led the Archdiocese since 2005.

My paternal grandmother was a gracious woman who lived to be 90 years old. Before she passed, she lost her eyesight but lived her final few years surrounded by family in our Nablus residence.

Chapter One: Palestine — A Childhood with Conflict

With Archbishop Atalla, Atlanta, 2013

My paternal grandparents (Priest Nicola and Grandma, Haniyya)

My grandfather, Nicola Bishara Khoury, the first priest of St. George's Greek Orthodox Church in Nisf Jubeil

My father and grandfather, Nisf Jubeil, circa 1946

Chapter One: Palestine — A Childhood with Conflict

St. George's Greek Orthodox Church, Nisf Jubeil

Facing West. The picture overlooks St. George's Church. The blue gate is the gate of the church's front yard. Behind the gate is the burial site of my grandparents: Nicola Khoury and his wife, Haniyya.

Village of Nisf Jubeil, 1935. Red dot points to the family home where my father was born in 1919

My father's name was Qustandi (the Arabic word for Constantine). Inspired by his faith, my grandfather granted most of his children Christian names. My father and his siblings lived almost their entire lives in the Middle East and among Muslims with peace, harmony, and mutual respect.

After their marriage in 1955, my parents raised a family of four — two boys and two girls. I was the youngest in the family. All our names were derived from the Arabic language: Hani, Samar, Hania, and Nabil. Nabil, my brother, was the oldest, followed by Hania, my older sister, then Samar, my younger sister. Motivated by Arabic tradition and culture, my parents believed that their children would be growing up in the Middle East, and therefore Arabic names would be most appropriate. That never happened. All of us ended up emigrating to Western countries. What an irony!

Chapter One: Palestine — A Childhood with Conflict   15

The four of us

Wedding picture of my parents, Qustandi Nicola Khoury & Laurice Lutfi Taqtaq, 1955

16 Giving Up Is Not An Option

Mother with my maternal grandmother, 1954

Grandmother, father, mother, siblings and me, Christmas Day, 1965

Chapter One: Palestine — A Childhood with Conflict   17

Christmas with siblings and cousins; circa 1969; I appear at the upper left corner telling everyone: shshshsh... (Be quiet!)

My sister Samar had SMA as well, but her disease progressed much slower than mine. Scientists believe that the disease develops much slower in females than in males. She has been living in Belgium since 1990.

My last name, as mentioned earlier, is the Arabic word for "priest." In the Christian Greek Orthodox tradition, when a priest has been ordained, the family's last name must officially thereafter reflect the priesthood, and on all legal documents, the family's name would forever change to Khoury. Prior to that, the family's name was Abu Smair. (This is like the Hebrew tradition with the family name Cohen.) My last name became an identifier of my religious background. In a predominantly Muslim society, I was easily recognized as being a member of the Christian faith.

Growing up under the Israeli occupation made it almost impossible for a person in public to celebrate their national identity as a Palestinian.

Raising the Palestinian flag was considered a crime. Demonstrating against the Israeli occupation could send the demonstrator to prison. Resisting occupation via armed struggle was dealt with as a form of terrorism punishable by a life sentence (Israeli law does not recognize the death penalty).

This reality was overshadowed by other forms or notions of identity — mainly social and religious — based on wealth, family name, religious affiliation, educational level, and even status stemming from whether you had a city or a country upbringing.

Elementary and Middle School

After spending one year at Beit Al-Tifel School, I transferred to Ibn-Qutaybah Elementary and Preparatory School, named after a prominent Muslim scholar, known for his work in literature, poetry, philosophy, and secular education. Beit Al-Tifel was only a K-1 school and its mission focused primarily on early development of children.

My new school was farther away from my house than the previous one had been. School busing was not available to anyone enrolled in public schools in Nablus during that time. It's worth noting again that the territory was under an Israeli military occupation that deprived Palestinians of all basic tenets of a normal life.

My mother decided that it would be beneficial for me to repeat the first grade at my new school for me to have a sound academic preparation. I repeated the first grade, and I had Mr. Abu Mohammed as my first-grade teacher at Ibn-Qutaybah. The word "Abu" is used for the combined words "father of." In Arab societies, a father and mother with a son or a daughter are nicknamed using "Abu" or "Um." For instance, if I had a son named Ibrahim, others would call me "Abu Ibrahim," father of Ibrahim. My wife would be called "Um Ibrahim," mother of Ibrahim. The label usually references the name of the eldest son or daughter. This was primarily a practice in Arab societies recognizing the significance of having children, especially having an elder son to carry the family name. This practice has roots and cultural and religious traditions.

My first day at Ibn Qutaybah's school was unpleasant. My mother and I arrived at the principal's office early in the morning. Mom went through the registration process as we sat in the office of Mr. Abu Iyad and she briefed him about my disability. She explained to him that I would not be able to play any kind of sports. The principal then directed me to my classroom at the end of a long corridor. I began walking toward the classroom very slowly as I limped from side to side. Watching her from a distance on her way out of school, I burst into tears, screaming "Please, please mama, don't go home and leave me here!" With the principal's help and encouragement, I was able to calm down and go to my classroom, where I was greeted by my teacher, Abu Muhammad, who seated me kindly in the desk nearest the door.

The school had two educational levels with grades 1 through 9. The first six grades constituted the elementary phase, while grades 7-9 constituted the preparatory phase. My older brother had just finished his ninth grade and left for secondary school. He was eight years older than I.

From my earliest years, I have thoroughly enjoyed learning. Education became for me a kind of escape, and it provided me, simultaneously, with the means to answer all types of questions that were popping up in my head such as: "Will I be able to further my education?", "What's going to happen to my health as I get older?", "What are my options in life?" I asked. I finally acknowledged and embraced the realization that I was and very likely would remain physically different.

My mother's reassurance and simple logic have motivated me all my life. Throughout the years, her wisdom and her words have sustained me almost beyond belief. "Something has been taken away from you, Hani," she would say, "but in return you have been given a special gift — you are very smart." I knew how difficult it was for her to witness me growing weaker and weaker, year after year. It must have been devastating for her as a mother.

"Where is God and why did he make me different?" I asked repeatedly. God, I had been taught, was divine and resided in heaven and we are "his" creation. I was told that God created the universe and wanted the best for "his" creation. God was, is, and forever will be able and willing to help people in the fight of good against evil, if we only believe. I heard this from nearly everyone in the society I grew up in, and especially at school. Denying God or having dissenting views about God would place a person in the category of infidels and nonbelievers. I believed in God (Jesus) as a child and in my youth, but I wasn't sure why! Was it hope or was it fear? Hope would allow me to believe that I might someday become physically able; fear, however, was much less accommodating. Although Jesus is the manifestation of God for Christians, he is not God (Allah) or his manifestation for Muslims. Although I was placed very early in the category of believers, my beliefs today reflect the values of a secular humanist.

I was not able to accept the explanations behind the use of religious interpretations by others to unfold the complexity of my own life. Luckily, I was growing up during a time when scientific explorations and inventions were sweeping the earth. I was growing up alongside a technological revolution with all kinds of possibilities for me and for countless others, with and without physical disabilities.

As the years went by and my physical condition continued to decline, I had to rely on a taxi for my daily commute to and from school. Almost every taxi driver became aware of my physical condition. My house was slightly off the main road. Some drivers were nice enough to drop me off at the doorstep. They would go the extra mile for me, as we say here in America. Others refused, forcing me to take the few extra steps. This disparity in behaviors I saw led me to question the humanitarian spirit in some people.

Chapter One: Palestine — A Childhood with Conflict

My parents were not able to afford buying a car, even a used one. Cars were very expensive due to an outrageously high import tax that was imposed on buyers by the Israeli government, which had control over almost every aspect of our lives. The Israeli occupation, presented as a security measure, placed severe restrictions on economic and financial institutions. Salaries and wages were extremely low during a time of political and economic uncertainty.

Moving to higher-level grades in school, I became more aware of the political conditions that surrounded me and of the society in which I was living. The older I got, the more I began to realize that we were under occupation, possibly for decades to come. I became politically mature at that young age. Not only politically mature, I began questioning the justification of the Israeli occupation based on Biblical interpretations. There seemed to be a clear contradiction between Judaism as a narrative of justice and the Israeli occupation as a tool of oppression. Religion must never be utilized in any shape or form as a means to impose injustice on others; therefore, secular beliefs began to emerge in my own way of thinking about the reality confronting me as a person with a disability who was also living under a military occupation, an occupation that has been justified by the occupier exploiting religious pretexts.

Israeli soldiers were routinely patrolling the streets of Nablus, near my house and school, on the roads within the city and between cities. They were everywhere. The occupation was still recent and maintaining control and avoiding any lapses in security made the military presence noticeable daily. Israel began to rule without mercy. Under occupation, Palestinians began to resist. Israel, however, insisted on ruling the occupied territories with an iron fist and a thirst for power and expansion. The world was becoming a dangerous place, greatly diminished in size, and my own world was now limited to my immediate neighborhood.

My Neighborhood

My friends in the neighborhood used to visit me at home, and my favorite time was when we played with marbles. Although I could not walk, I was able to crawl on my hands and knees. I had several friends and lots of marbles. One day I'd lose a few marbles and on the next day I'd win some. We even fought over marbles during our games, jealous of who had more, both in number and in intriguing design. Those of us with lots of marbles used to organize and lead the neighborhood in marble matches. I stayed away from other games that required physical strength, managing only to watch.

Near my house lived another Christian family, the Taweel family — Mr. Daoud (David), his wife Raymonda and their four children: Diana, Hala, Suha, and their only son, Gabby. They were extremely pleasant. Hala was my age and Suha was two years older. Both Diana and Gabby were quite a bit older than I so I did not mingle with them. I used to wait on the balcony of my house for Hala or Suha to go outside and play. On many occasions I would just walk very slowly to their house, chatting with them as I watched them play.

Their mother, Mrs. Taweel, is a well-known Palestinian journalist. She had frequent visitors from all over the world. In addition to Arabic, she was fluent in English and French. Mr. Taweel was educated at Oxford University and was a calm man and a successful banker. Mrs. Taweel was active in the community and on the political scene. She was imprisoned several times by the Israeli authorities for her outspoken views on the Israeli occupation. Admired by many people in the community, her love for Palestine was, and remains, evident. She is the author of *My Home, My Prison* published in 1980.

Mrs. Taweel managed to build a volleyball court in her backyard and opened it to all the teenagers in the neighborhood. Adjacent to their house was a Melkite Catholic Church and Father Habra was the priest during that time. I can recall how mean he was! He was so protective of the church's premises that every time the volleyball landed in the

Chapter One: Palestine — A Childhood with Conflict

church's yard, he would take out a knife, drive it through the ball, and kick it back over the fence into the court. Mrs. Taweel would go out and scream at Father Habra. Occasionally she took off in her car to buy another volleyball for the kids in the neighborhood so that they could continue playing. This incident repeated itself several times! A few years later, the Taweel family moved to the city of Ramallah, and I learned later that Suha married the Chairman of the Palestine Liberation Organization (PLO), Yasser Arafat.

The Mediterranean Sea

On several occasions, my father, living with limited financial resources, had to borrow a car from his relatives or close friends to run family errands or take a daytrip with the family. On occasion he would borrow the car to take the family swimming in the Mediterranean Sea, inside Israel proper (Israel within the 1948 border). One of the two beaches that I clearly remember was in Natanya, a coastal city; the other, Mikhmoret Beach (Mikhmoret is the Hebrew word for a "fishing net") was a little north of Natanya. On the way back home from the beach, we would stop at an ice cream shop alongside the road.

Those were the happy days, and whenever we were at the beach, Palestinians and Israelis alike were having fun away from the political scene. The beaches were the very places where national origin had little or no significance. There were Palestinians, but mostly Israelis, playing frisbee, flying kites, fishing, or playing volleyball on the clean sandy beaches. Those were the only times when the so-called "enemies" turned into "semi-friends." There were those who were suspicious of Palestinians speaking Arabic on Israeli beaches where the predominantly spoken language was Hebrew; these places existed outside of the political landscape reminding all of us that there is such a thing as common humanity.

Not being able to swim, I had to rely on an inflated tire tube to stay afloat in the wavy waters of the Mediterranean. Every time I got near someone who spoke Hebrew, I would say "Shalom," the Hebrew word for peace. On those beaches I learned the basics of Hebrew, which was not taught in Palestinian schools during that time.

It was on those beaches that Israeli society appeared as a mosaic of many different traditions, languages, and nationalities. People spoke Arabic, Hebrew, Polish, English, German, Russian, and French, among still other languages. Many of them were probably the survivors, or descendants of survivors, of the Holocaust, while others could have been settlers living in the occupied territories or young soldiers serving in the Israeli military that was brutally occupying those territories and terrifying the Palestinian people. Israeli society was truly a mosaic of different cultures.

Those peaceful days full of open multicultural encounters were contrasted by the cruel irony which was taking place in plain sight. Jews worldwide were invited to come to Israel and become citizens of the state. This was part of Zionism and the Zionist agenda, which proved to be at the expense of Palestinian human and national rights (Beit-Hallahmi, 1993).

Mikhmoret, a coastal Jewish settlement, was built in 1945 on lands belonging to Palestinians south of the village of Arab al-Nufay'at. "On 10 April 1948, the Haganah [the main Zionist paramilitary organization operating covertly during the British Mandate for Palestine] ordered the villagers to leave, and the village itself was demolished by the end of April and early May" (Zochrot, 'Arab al-Nufay'at 2014).

The Search for Answers

As I grew older and matured, searching for answers to my own questions became more intense. The notions of personhood, cosmology, disability, and identity (social, political, religious) required much more understanding on my part.

At the end of my elementary and preparatory schooling at the age of fifteen, I clearly understood that society at large, including my family and friends, perceived me as being physically different and that my future would be in jeopardy if alternatives were not sought. I was asking, "Will I be able to go to university? How can I achieve independence, both physically and financially? Will I ever be able to have a family of my own?"

The Israeli occupation had no regard to the native Palestinian population, and the agenda of what amounted to ethnic cleansing was well on its way (Pappe, 2015). As a person born with a physical disability, I was denied social, political, and human rights that could have made my life easier to navigate. In a way, I was being pushed to leave my homeland in search of a place that would recognize my human dignity, and rights.

The Social and Religious Contexts of Disability

It became clear to me early on that those social and religious values and traditions played a significant role in the development of people's attitudes toward me and toward each other in general. Islam by its very own nature consists of a comprehensive theology. It is a system of life that derives its laws from the Quran and the life of Prophet Mohammed. Mercy is at the pinnacle of Islamic beliefs about God (Allah). I felt like I was surrounded by people everywhere (home, school, and on the street) who were praying for my physical salvation, hopeful that God would grant me physical amnesty or wholeness through a miracle, or through his mercy. In Islam, surrendering to the will of God is in essence what it means to be a Muslim. God created me and God would take care of me in his own way. In that culture, I became, through the will of God, an object of compassion.

The Christian perspective was slightly different. God was responsible for my creation, but my deliverance would come out of my acceptance of my own suffering rather than an acceptance of the will of God —accept your disability and the suffering it brings. My acceptance of the outcomes, including pain and anguish in all its forms, would be sufficient alone to pave the road for my salvation. In a way, life would become complete, meaningful, and purposeful through the graceful acceptance of my own fate.

For believers in God, whether devout Muslims or Christians, I could find sympathy and hope through the lens of a magnificent, merciful, and powerful creator — God (Allah for Muslims and Jesus Christ for Christians) — but for the rest of society, my gateway to overcome my disability and to prosper lay not in the magnificence of a merciful God but on my own efforts. I could overcome and prosper "only if" I had what it takes to "overcome" for myself. For those without a purely religious perspective, I was an object of admiration through the comparative personal lenses of ability versus disability. Dependency on a divine power for my salvation was absent from such a perspective. It was a matter of the struggle between ability and disability. My "salvation," as it were, was all up to me.

In such a culture, a person born with a severe physical disability was expected to remain at home to be taken care of by family members and society. Using adaptive equipment such as wheelchairs or crutches was seen as a sign of weakness deserving of pity or shame. Difference and diversity were seldom seen as sources of such things as strength, alternative perspectives, pluralism, and acceptance through insight.

Searching for answers to intricate questions was never easy for me. Looking for explanations had to go beyond God, politics, and attitudes. Philosophical and theological frameworks could not respond adequately to my immediate concerns or questions, nor did they provide me with instant solutions to my immediate need to survive. "To endure" is sometimes the only answer we have.

As I approached my late teens, I noticed feelings of guilt experienced by my parents, especially my father. He began to feel responsible for bringing a child into the world with such serious physical issues. I began to witness those feelings as I entered the secondary phase of my schooling. The older I got, the more intense my father's feelings became. I was getting noticeably weaker, and the uncertainty

Chapter One: Palestine — A Childhood with Conflict

surrounding my future was increasing. I could no longer carry out even routine physical activities, such as dressing or bathing. Climbing stairs was no longer possible, and public transportation was no longer feasible, for the simple reason that I could no longer stand up without assistance.

I spent a total of nine years at Ibn Qutaybah School. During those years, my physical condition deteriorated significantly. I could still walk very short distances, but always with great difficulty. Relying on a wheelchair was not an option without upper-body strength. Electric wheelchairs were not available or affordable, but even if a wheelchair had been an option, I would have feared the bullying I most likely would have had to endure. The culture of Palestine and the Arab world in general placed a stigma on those who did not fit the "norm" including those with physical disabilities. This stigma, fueled by fear and ignorance, led to perceiving others as inferiors, which children viewed as permission to engage in name calling and ridiculing.

The Political Context

During those nine years, and when I was in eighth grade, I remember the signing of the Camp David peace accords between Israel and Egypt. Egypt had lost the Sinai desert to Israel during the 1967 war. The peace treaty had ensured the return of the Sinai desert to Egyptian rule in return for normalized relations between Egypt and Israel. The West Bank and the Gaza Strip were supposed to be part of that agreement, but last-minute complications and pressures on the Egyptian delegation negotiating at Camp David forced Egyptian president Anwar Sadat to take a unilateral approach to peace with Israel. Sadat's action angered Palestinians living in the West Bank and Gaza, as well as the exiled Palestinian leadership, the PLO in Lebanon, and all the Arab states.

Along with my parents, I watched with curiosity and skepticism the first visit to Israel of the first head of an Arab state. Peace efforts, however, did not spill over to the West Bank. Consequently, Israel's policies to build and expand settlements in the West Bank and East

Jerusalem began to intensify as they were inhabited by extremists (Adiv & Schwartz, 1992). Egypt was removed from the Arab world and from the minds of those who condemned the idea of unilateral peace.

Entering my secondary education phase brought with it a critical turning point. Confronting the reality of the Israeli occupation and Israel's policies of discrimination began to impact my life significantly. Palestinians under occupation were dehumanized. They were suffering from land confiscations, curfews, roadblocks, blockades, deportations, imprisonment, home demolitions, collective punishment, deliberate destruction of agricultural land and olive trees by settlers, travel restrictions, the building of new settlements and the expanding of older ones, diverting water supplies to settlements—the list goes on.

Such practices took place in the name of the state's sovereignty over land it had occupied, contrary to the word, wisdom, and the spirit of international law. The aims of Zionism at establishing a "homeland" for the Jewish people were finally accomplished in 1948. However, the appetite for expanding that homeland has never ceased to exist.

Israeli historian and scholar Meron Benvenisti described the tragedy of demolishing Palestinian homes in an article he wrote in the Israeli newspaper Ha'Aretz.

It would be hard to overstate the symbolic value of a house to an individual for whom the culture of wandering and of becoming rooted to the land is so deeply engrained in tradition, for an individual whose national mythos is based on the tragedy of being uprooted from a stolen homeland. The arrival of a firstborn son and the building of a home are the central events in such an individual's life because they symbolize continuity in time and physical space. And with the demolition of the individual's home comes the destruction of the world. (Banvenisti, 2002)

Given that I could not participate with my fellow students in any of the demonstrations against the Israeli occupation, I had to sit and watch

Chapter One: Palestine — A Childhood with Conflict

from the sidelines as these discriminatory policies and practices of Israel were carried out. Such policies and practices reflected Israeli power as a precondition for survival and to be understood as a collective struggle to bring about God's will (Ezrahi, 1999). I was disheartened and furious. My sense of justice demanded my participation, but my physical disability stood in the way.

My high school education began in the 10th grade at King Talal's Secondary School in Nablus. The school was named after King Talal bin Abdullah, King of Jordan from 1951 to 1952. I remained in that school for one year as a 10th grader. During that year, at the age of sixteen, I experienced firsthand the brutality of the Israeli occupation.

Palestinians living throughout the West Bank and Gaza, especially older students, were known for commemorating national holidays such as Land Day, which has been celebrated on March 30 every year since 1976. On that date and in response to the Israeli government's decision to confiscate thousands of acres belonging to Palestinian Arabs living inside Israel, a major confrontation between Arab citizens of Israel and Israeli police took place and led to the death of six unarmed Arab Israeli citizens and the wounding or arresting of hundreds of others. This was not the only day during which students in my school demonstrated against the Israeli occupation, but on that day, shortly before I turned sixteen, students began to throw rocks at passing Israeli settler cars, with their yellow license plates, and military jeeps patrolling the area near the school. Israeli settlers throughout the occupied territories could carry arms authorized by the Israeli government. Most settlers were armed with Uzis, M16s, or pistols. Reacting to rock throwers, Israeli settlers fired warning shots to scare off demonstrating students. Whenever the attempt failed, the Israeli soldiers would be called to the scene and different plans would be implemented by the army. Among the tactics used was the use of water cannons with colored ink to leave a mark on students' clothing for later identification and arrests.

Israeli soldiers would surround the school and use tear gas to dispel student crowds of rock-throwers in what could have turned at any moment into deadly confrontations. I remained seated in my own desk in the classroom during what became a chaotic situation. Luckily no live bullets or tear gas were aimed toward my classroom.

Suddenly, Israeli soldiers, coming from every possible direction and through every school gate, invaded the school. In groups of four or five, they entered every classroom in search of rock-throwers, demanding that students stand up immediately. Soldiers then identified and arrested those who were suspected of throwing rocks. Upon entering my classroom, four soldiers and their commander ordered all of us to stand. As I was trying with great difficulty to obey the order to stand, one of the soldiers ran toward me, grabbed my shoulder, and slapped me in the face shouting in Arabic "Waqif ya haywan," which means "Stand up, you animal!" (Most Israeli soldiers serving in the occupied territories had already mastered basic fluency in Arabic.)

During such moments, teachers could only watch helplessly and defenselessly against heavily armed soldiers. I still remember my teacher screaming at the soldier, "Leave him! Leave him alone! He has a physical disability!" At that moment, I looked into the soldier's eyes as he looked into mine. Although he could have said he was sorry, he could not bring himself to say it. After all, soldiers learn only how to fight. An apology would have been a sign of weakness and an acknowledgment of wrongdoing. At that moment, I felt that both of us were looking for words, but they were nowhere to be found. I was shocked, humiliated, and dehumanized. I could not tell what went through that soldier's head, but the arrogance of power seemed to have taken over. What happened to me that day was nothing compared to what other students had to endure — beatings, torture, and imprisonment. Dehumanizing the Palestinian people was at the forefront of Israeli decision makers to justify their policies of oppression and discrimination in the eyes of the world.

"What have I done to deserve all this?" I asked. Nothing around me made any sense. My human value was diminished in front of my own eyes, not only by society and its attitudes, but also by a relentless and ruthless Israeli occupation. My thirst for justice increased over the years and for obvious reasons, but my efforts to find answers to a myriad of questions threatened to endanger my own sanity and well-being.

During that same year and after I reached my 16th birthday, my father was told about an Israeli law that would allow parents of children with disabilities to import cars and be exempted from paying an outrageously high import tax. He learned later that this law was applicable only to Israeli citizens, but I remember how excited we were as a family about the possibility of being able to purchase a tax-exempt vehicle that would allow my parents to drive me back and forth to school. Shortly after my birthday, my father applied to the military headquarters in Beit El near the city of Ramallah to purchase a car. A few weeks later he was summoned for an interview with an Israeli official at Beit El regarding the application. After a brief introduction and during the interview, the official asked my father, "You're asking the Israeli government to grant you a tax exemption, right Mr. Khoury?" "Yes," my father replied. The official then looked at my father and asked, "And what have you done for Israel, Mr. Khoury?" To that my father replied, "Nothing, nothing at all, and there is not a thing I would do for an occupying state." The official looked again at my father and said, "Application denied."[2]

The Human Context

Living in a predominantly Muslim society was peaceful and respectful. After all, Nablus is well-known for the harmony between its inhabitants: Muslims, Christians, and Samaritans. It's that diversity that I believe made the city a cradle of peaceful coexistence. After all, people living in the West Bank and the Gaza Strip saw themselves as the first victims of military occupation.

---

[2] For a detailed and complete understanding of the wider Zionist-Arab conflict leading to the Israeli-Palestinian dispute, I highly recommend Benny Morris's *Righteous victims, a history of the Zionist-Arab conflict, 1881-2001* (2001).

I can remember well the wonderful relationship my family had with Muslim friends and neighbors. My relationships with my friends and teachers were as exemplary as anyone could ever imagine.

In 1980, while I was in the 10th grade at King Talal high school, my father traveled to Beirut, Lebanon following the sudden death of my uncle there, not surprising for a man in his 70s. During that time, I was completely dependent on my father to take me back and forth to school daily and to carry me on his back from the car to my classroom desk.

After my father left for Lebanon, my mother took it upon herself to drive me back and forth to school. The janitor of the school, a pious Muslim, took it upon himself to carry me on his back from the car to my desk in the classroom. When we were dismissed in the afternoon, he carried me back to the car. The janitor committed himself to do this for an entire week for my sake. Differences of faith did not stand in the way of Palestinians treating each other with mutual respect and human dignity. His very actions confirmed the existence of human values within the Islamic faith. My best and closest friends were Muslims, and during that time there was no friction whatsoever between the members of the same society. The national identity was the predominant identity.

The Victims of Tragedy

In Jerusalem there is a memorial for the victims of the Nazi Holocaust. Foreign dignitaries and heads of state pay respect to the souls of millions of Jews whose living bodies were turned into ashes by the evil of Nazi atrocities. Yad Vashem is a memorial honoring the Jewish victims of Nazi atrocities. The Law of Yad Vashem in the Israeli Knesset (Parliament) to build the memorial was passed in 1953. Across from that memorial lie the Palestinian victims of Deir Yassin.

> Early on the morning of Friday, April 9th, 1948, the beautiful Arab village of Deir Yassin on the west side of Jerusalem was attacked by commandos of the Irgun and the Stern Gang. More than 100 men, women and children were systematically killed. Within a year the

village had been repopulated with orthodox Jewish immigrants from Poland, Romania and Slovakia. Its cemetery was bulldozed, and its name wiped off the map. The massacre of Deir Yassin marked the beginning of the depopulation of more than 400 Arab villages and the exile of more than 700,000 Palestinians. (Deir Yassin remembered 2018)

Learning about the Holocaust in Europe under Nazi rule was not taught at Palestinian schools. Arabs and Muslims across the world felt no responsibility for what happened to European Jews at the hands of "Christians." On the contrary, there is recognition among many Jews worldwide that Arabs and Muslims welcomed them to their homelands during such times as the Spanish Inquisition. As a result, school curricula covering historical events in Europe did not cover the Holocaust in any depth. It was rarely mentioned or detailed as a historical event.

But the Holocaust became a central event in Jewish thought and afterwards in the establishment of Israel. There are those (Norman Finkelstein, for example) who argue that the Holocaust was used for political reasons to garnish support for the Jewish state at the expense of both traditional Jewish values and native Palestinians, especially after the 1967 war. The Holocaust, he argued, was used to justify Israel's brutal occupation of Palestinian lands as Israel was distancing itself from the rules of international law. Finkelstein argued as well that exploiting Jewish suffering for political reasons does not reflect Jewish moral traditions (Finkelstein, 2015).

Theologian Marc Ellis argued for a theology of liberation stemming from thoughtful and rich Jewish interpretations of the Jewish past and thirst for justice applicable to all humankind. Such interpretations, he argued, were absent from Israel's treatment of the Palestinian people who were either expelled or came under Israeli occupation. Both scholars have essentially argued that Judaism does not equate with Israel.³

Ideology, coupled with the arrogance of power, control, and expansion, has trumped the moral future of what has become, in the eyes of many people throughout the world, an incredible modern state that has rejected in its actions the possibility of a lasting peace in a two-state solution, one for the Palestinians, the other for Israelis. Those obstacles to peace included the building and expanding of Jewish settlements in occupied land, rejecting the notion of Jerusalem as one capital for two peoples, and rejecting the "right of return" for those who were expelled from their homes and land in 1948.

Who am I to say that Israeli policies and actions are moving in the wrong direction? Only those with long-term vision and long-lasting political and/or military insights can testify to that. There are many Israelis and Jews around the globe who would testify to that scary thought. Uri Avnery, who served as a member in the Israeli Knesset for almost a decade and who fought for the establishment of Israel in 1948 as a member of the Irgun militia, is one of them. He is a writer and founder of the peace movement in Israel, Gush Shalom. He has taught many about the need for carefully examining politics and history in an age of political uncertainty, ideological absolutism, and abuse of power. Uri Avnery passed away in 2018, but I urge everyone to read his articles published at http://uriavnery.com/en/.

As I was growing up in Nablus, and as I wrote earlier, I received my knowledge about current events through the media, but also as an observer of events around me. My father used to listen to the BBC (British Broadcasting Company) as a source of news and coverage of current events. I don't remember much from the 1967 war, but I remember more about the 1973 Yom Kippur (Ramadan) War and the 1982 Israeli invasion of Lebanon.

---

³ Much Earlier, Rabbi Elmer Berger explored the relationship between Judaism and Jewish nationalism in his book *Judaism or Jewish Nationalism, the Alternative to Zionism*, published, 1957.

Chapter One: Palestine — A Childhood with Conflict

Palestinians who resisted Israel's occupation through armed struggle were labeled as "terrorists." In Israeli media, that was a common portrayal of those who believed that they were fighting for their freedom and independence. Palestinians adopted all means available to resist Israeli occupation of the West Bank and Gaza and retaliated against Israeli aggression. Some even fought against Israel's right to exist, citing historical, political, and moral illegitimacies. Undoubtedly, some of those means were violent while others were peaceful. Innocent people on both sides were endlessly caught in vicious cycles of action and retaliation. Humanity became the true and real victim in this conflict. Palestinians and Israelis are human beings. They deserve to live their lives in peace and dignity as equals in humanity. However, for this to be realized there must be an understanding that two wrongs, although unequal in impact, never make a right. There is a moral equivalency (in its most tragic sense) between the killing of a single life and the destruction of life itself. Palestinian violence, legitimized by resistance as a legal means to fight occupation and oppression, reached innocent Israelis, also seen as occupiers and agents of settler colonialism and imperialism. On the other hand, Israeli extremism, and apartheid-like policies against Palestinians, before and after 1948, were also reaching and killing Palestinians directly or indirectly. An increasing number of Israelis and Jews around the world (although far from being a critical mass) began to show and express their harsh criticism of Israeli policies and practices, comparable to those found in South Africa during the apartheid regime.

In his recent book, distinguished historian Walter H. Hixon writes:

Until relatively recently, support for Israel was virtually inseparable from American Jewish identity. However, in recent years it has become clear that while the majority of American Jews continue to embrace, as they have long done, a liberal worldview, a minority of wealthy, older, and mostly Orthodox Jews are more-right wing. Their wealth anchors unconditional US support for Israel even as the Zionist state carries out aggressive and illegal policies. The gulf between majority liberal American-Jewish opinion on one side, and

Israeli aggression backed by a right-wing minority of American Jews on the other, constitutes an escalating "crisis of Zionism." (Hixson, 2021)

There are immense contributions to humanity by courageous Jewish thinkers. Their voices of human consciousness speak truth to Israeli abuse of power and Palestinian human rights. They have addressed the key aspects of the modern conflict in the Middle East between Arabs and Jews which is nearly 100 years old. To some extent, Jews are slightly divided when it comes to Jewish ethical tradition vis-a-vis the moral future of Israel and key elements for its survival.

There is equal division among the Palestinians about the future of peace with Israel, given the intransigent policies of successive Israeli governments. Jewish scholars, philosophers, journalists, and human rights activists like Noam Chomsky, Hannah Arendt, Norman Finkelstein, Sara Roy, Ellen Siegel, Marc Ellis, Ilan Pappe, Max Blumenthal, Martin Buber, Felicia Langer, Gideon Levy, Daniel Barenboim and many more have taken it upon themselves to explain to the world the challenges facing Jewish identity. They have outlined the injustices which have been inflicted on the Palestinian people by the creation of a Jewish state in Palestine. They have also strongly argued against Israel's continued occupation of Palestine.

In remembering the late Edward Said during a 2008 lecture at the University of Adelaide in Australia, Sara Roy, a Senior Research Scholar at the Center for Middle Eastern Studies at Harvard University, said:

Israel's occupation of the Palestinians is not the moral equivalent of the Nazi genocide of the Jews. It does not have to be. The fact that it is not in no way tempers the brutality of the repression, which has become frighteningly normal. Occupation is about the domination and dispossession of one people by another. It is about the destruction of their property and the destruction of their soul. At its core, occupation aims to deny Palestinians their humanity by

Chapter One: Palestine — A Childhood with Conflict

denying them the right to determine their existence, to live normal lives in their own homes. And just as there is no moral equivalence or symmetry between the Holocaust and the occupation, so there is no moral equivalence or symmetry between the occupier and the occupied, no matter how much we as Jews regard ourselves as victim. (Roy, 2019)

Continued Israeli military occupation of the West Bank, East Jerusalem, the Gaza Strip, and the Golan Heights for decades gave momentum to the rise of not only secular Palestinian liberation movements, but also of religious fundamentalism in the Middle East, both Jewish and Islamic. In the Middle East, religious fundamentalism was on the rise. In the West, especially in Europe and the United States, the Christian right and pro-Israel ultra-conservative forces continued to dominate the political scene and maintained a stronghold on foreign policy. Most notable is the powerful pro-Israel lobby that exists across the United States, but especially on Capitol Hill. This lobby has shaped and influenced US foreign policy in the Middle East, before and after the creation of Israel in 1948 (Tivnan, 1987).

Too much effort and capital were invested by the Israeli lobby in the Western World to create an image of a heroic reality of unprecedented religious and political advances. If you want to carry out an unjust deed on others, all you must do is dehumanize the oppressed in the eyes of the world, and there is a good probability that you will get away with it. This is precisely what happened to Jews under Nazi rule in Germany and throughout Europe. Jews were also dehumanized in the eyes of their persecutors.

As I had tried to do with the Holocaust, I tried to remember my first real encounter with the [Israeli] occupation. One of the earliest was a scene I witnessed standing on a street with some Palestinian friends. An elderly man was walking along leading his donkey. A small child of no more than three or four, clearly his grandson, was with him. All of a sudden some nearby Israeli soldiers approached the old man and stopped him. One of them went over to the donkey and pried open its mouth. "Old man," he asked, "why are your donkey's teeth so yellow? Don't you brush your donkey's teeth?" The old Palestinian was mortified, the little boy visibly upset. The soldier repeated his question, yelling this time, while the other soldiers laughed. The child began to cry, and the old man just stood there silently, humiliated. As the scene continued a crowd gathered. The soldier then ordered the old man to stand behind the donkey and demanded that he kiss the animal's behind. At first, the old man refused but as the soldier screamed at him and his grandson became hysterical, he bent down and did it. The soldiers laughed and walked away. We all stood there in silence, ashamed to look at each other, the only sound the sobs of the little boy. The old man, demeaned and destroyed, did not move for what seemed a very long time.

I stood in stunned disbelief. I immediately thought of the stories my parents had told me of how Jews had been treated by the Nazis in the 1930s, before the ghettos and death camps, of how Jews would be forced to clean sidewalks with toothbrushes and have their beards cut off in public. What happened to the old man was equivalent in principle, intent, and impact: to humiliate and dehumanize. Throughout that summer of 1985, I saw similar incidents: young Palestinian men stopped in the streets by Israeli soldiers and forced to bark like dogs on their hands and knees or sometimes to dance. (Roy, 2019)

Virtually all colonial powers have utilized this very effective tactic at one time or another. Of course, there were acts of violence committed by Palestinians, but those violent acts were strategically positioned to create an image in the eyes and minds of Western societies of the Orientalist: a savage who does not understand or appreciate self-determination or rightful independence. (Said, 2004)

Chapter One: Palestine — A Childhood with Conflict

The Strength To Contemplate A Future Elsewhere

There were mainly two reasons that pushed me and my parents to take a critical step in my life. Given the political climate and a progressive physical disability, looking for a future elsewhere became as essential as survival itself.

The Israeli policies toward Palestinians in general, and toward me as a person with a disability, were blatant actions of discrimination. I was never imprisoned or tortured, but many Palestinians were. Since 1967, Israel has arrested and jailed around 800,000 Palestinians (according to estimates from the Palestinians' Ministry of Prisoners). According to Palestinian estimates, some 70% of Palestinian families have had one or more family members serve time in an Israeli prison for actions against the occupation.

In addition to military presence, mass arrests, and curfews, living in the occupied territories meant living for the most part under economic hardships, inequalities, and injustices. For example, Palestinians had to pay higher taxes compared to their Israeli counterparts (Hass, 2000).

One of the greatest ironies in my life is that as a Palestinian, I was oppressed by an Israeli occupation, but I was also greatly influenced, both academically and intellectually, by great secular Jewish thinkers, professors, theologians, and mentors, before and after my time as a student at Syracuse University.

Looking Back and Moving Forward: The Farewell

I spent my last two years in high school at Qadri Tuqan[4] High School, a school that is known for its science curriculum. After selling

---

[4] Qadri Tuqan was born in Nablus in 1911 and received his baccalaureate degree in mathematics from the American University of Beirut in 1929. He worked as a teacher in Nablus, was active in the Palestinian national movement, and was later

a piece of land, my dad was finally able to purchase a used vehicle (a French-made white Peugeot 404), which enabled him to become fully responsible for my daily commute to and from school.

Dad and I arrived at school early each morning at around 7:00 a.m. and discovered that the school janitor had already opened the school's gate for the car to get through to take me as close as possible to the classroom. My dad would then carry me on his back and set me at my desk. During the winter season, I had to endure the cold temperatures while remaining in the classroom for nearly eight hours where the only heat available was the body temperatures of nearly thirty students. My ability to walk was greatly diminished by the age of seventeen.

The focus of my last two years in high school was, of course, on learning and academic achievement. Although relatives from the United States and Canada had encouraged my parents to send me abroad to further my education, it was my father who taught me the greatest lesson, that even though we may lose our physical freedoms, no one can strip away our knowledge and understanding. That wisdom rang true to me from a very young age, knowing that although my freedoms will be limited by my disability, who and what I make of myself will always be up to me and will always transcend my limitations.

Waking up every morning and going to school was my priority every day. Regardless of the weather condition or the political climate, I woke up every day wanting to go to school as the idea of possibly moving to a different country became more feasible. My brother had just transferred from the American University of Beirut, where he was a student, to Syracuse University in New York due to a deteriorating civil war in Lebanon. Consequently, I began to entertain seriously the possibility that I might follow in his footsteps.

---

arrested by British authorities for his political activism. He co-founded An-Najah College in Nablus and served as head of its administration until 1950. (from Palestinian Academic Society for the Study of International Affairs – Jerusalem)

Chapter One: Palestine — A Childhood with Conflict

I knew at that time that my future would require me to use adaptive equipment such as a wheelchair, especially since I hoped and planned to attend college. America became well-known worldwide for its laws protecting the rights of people with disabilities. In addition, my brother had been studying and living in the US for several years. Naturally, America became the center of my family's attention.

I spent the last two years in high school learning mathematics, physics, chemistry, Arabic, English, and Arab social studies. As a Christian, Islamic religious studies as an academic subject were not a mandatory requirement. This was the case for me from kindergarten through twelfth grade.

On many occasions I remained in class during religious instruction and how thankful I am today for being able to do so. Islam, like Judaism and Christianity, has endless spiritual values comforting to the human soul and responsive to human suffering. Previously, while at Ibn Qutayba School, I was a student for several years of the great Samaritan teacher, Ismail Al-Samri. What a privilege it was! His love for science and his students left a long and lasting impression on me. He was disciplined, organized, compassionate, and made science an interesting and intriguing subject. Samaritans assert that their worship is the true religion of the ancient Israelites prior to the Babylonian Exile.

All my other teachers belonged to the Muslim faith. They also were teachers that have greatly encouraged me as a student. Their names are engraved in my memory: Bashir Maqboul, Fouzan Al-Jabi, Adel Hubaisheh, Omar Hamdan, Ibrahim Au O'bayya, Sami Salem, Omar Natour, Muhammad Shreideh, Lutfi Zaghloul. Mahmood Abo Al-Ezz and Muhammad Hamed. Sadly, several of them have passed away.

My relationship with my classmates during high school was amazing. My classmates were empathetic toward me and appreciative of my will and resolve to obtain a high school education. During lunch break, several of my friends would choose to remain in the classroom with me instead of venturing out to the schoolyard. We managed to socialize and talk about TV shows, homework assignments, and gossip about our teachers and other students. On several occasions we would have an early breakfast together. We took turns bringing in Hummus (chickpeas dip), Falafel (fried vegetable patties), and Foul Mudammas (fava beans dip), and of course fresh pita bread. Our favorite drink was hot tea. That was a type of monthly tradition at school; however, on days of political unrest and demonstrations, things were different. On several occasions my classmates rushed and carried me on their shoulders to safety in the principal's office to avoid injury from live ammunition or from inhaling tear gas.

Exposure to different religious and spiritual perspectives has helped me tremendously in the discovery of first-class qualities in all people and across all cultures and boundaries. I have learned from the diversity of religious perspectives that the fight of good against evil depends on the values instilled in every person for the sole purpose of protecting and nurturing human life.

On the bus during a high school trip to the Mediterranean Sea, May 1983

Chapter One: Palestine — A Childhood with Conflict

With my Arabic language teacher Mr. Omar Hamdan and a few classmates

My English language teacher Mr. Sami Salem and a few more classmates

On a school trip at the shores of the Mediterranean coastal city of Akka (Acre). My physics teacher, Mr. Omar Natour (left), My school principal, Mr. Deeb Mashaiekh (center left), my mathematics teacher, Mr. Fouzan Al-Jabi (center back), Qadri Tukan High School, May 1983

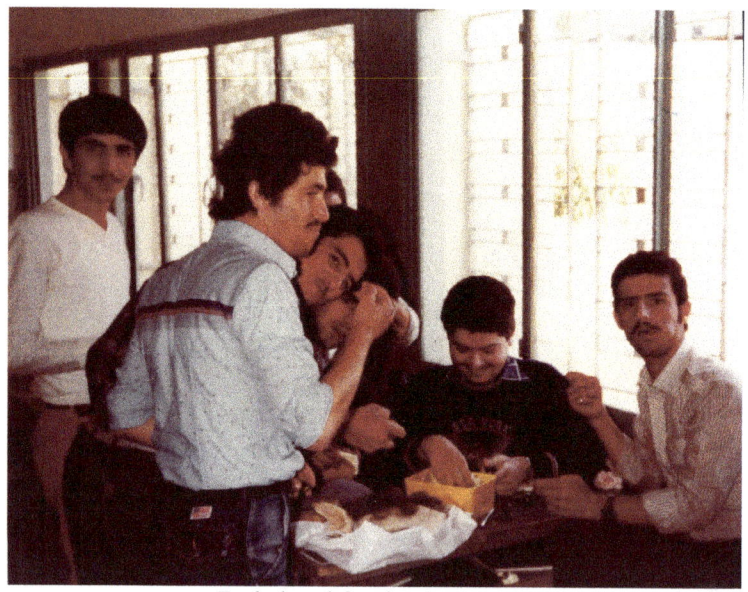

Early breakfast in class, 1983

Chapter One: Palestine — A Childhood with Conflict

My 12th grade classmates, 1983

Honoring the legacy of my Chemistry teacher, Mr. Muhammad Hamed in a ceremony at Al-Najah National University, 2017

Honoring the legacy of my Arabic Language teacher, the late Bashir Maqboul, Nablus, 2016

After graduation from high school in June of 1983, and after completing all the requirements for an F-1 visa allowing me to enter and reside in the United States as a student, I eagerly awaited my journey to a new world, a journey that drew nearer and nearer each day. I had to prepare myself to say goodbye to all my friends and even my pets at home. The excitement about the journey overcame my sadness of leaving behind everything I had known for eighteen years. A new opportunity was awaiting me on the horizon. An entire future became dependent on that once-in-a-lifetime opportunity. I even had a countdown of days remaining before I crossed the Jordan River with my parents for my departure from Queen Alia's International Airport in Amman, Jordan to JFK's International Airport in New York City. My new life abroad was about to begin.

Chapter Two: My Journey to America

Introduction

On August 12, 1983, I arrived at JFK international airport in New York City. Not knowing what to expect, I was determined to achieve all that I could in this country known as the United States of America. America was known worldwide to be the land of dreams and possibilities. On that day, I began a new phase in my life, determined to get a taste of whatever those dreams and possibilities might hold in store for someone like me.

Accompanied by my parents, I listened as the captain of the Royal Jordanian 747 jumbo jet announced on the intercom our preparation for landing. I remember seeing the amazing colorful, glowing, and sparkling lights of New York City's streets and skyscrapers, all through the plane's window. As we prepared for touchdown, I felt a blend of emotions. I was amazed, joyful, excited, happy, but those feelings were mixed with anxiety and apprehension. After all, life is a trial. Luckily the plane circled around the city a few times before final permission was granted for it to land, giving me ample time to think and reflect—and to calm down! There I was, 6000 miles away from my homeland in Palestine, about to embark on a journey that would lead me to places and present me with experiences that I could never, ever, have imagined. With an admission letter from Onondaga Community College (OCC) in Syracuse, I was able to enter the country on an F-1 student visa I had obtained at the American Consulate in East Jerusalem. Encouraged by many relatives living in the United States and Canada, and by the reassurances of my brother Nabil, I was finally ready to take this huge and long-hoped-for step.

Nabil was waiting for us at the airport with a rental car he had driven from Syracuse six hours away from New York City. He was attending Syracuse University (SU) after leaving the American University of Beirut due to the civil war erupting in the mid-70s in Lebanon. His intention was to attend SU in pursuit of both an undergraduate and a master's degree in civil engineering.

As we drove away from the airport heading back to Syracuse, only a few minutes into the drive, my father realized that as he was helping me into the car back at the airport, we had left our passports in the terminal. I remember still the heated argument that took place between my parents regarding my disability. Dad blamed Mom for forgetting the passports as she was instructing him on how to transfer me into the car from the wheelchair provided by the airline, the first wheelchair I had ever used. My brother immediately returned to the airport to the exact location where we believed our passports had been left. Fortunately, we found them at the airline counter nearest our parking spot, and we left again in the middle of the night toward Syracuse.

We arrived in Syracuse early in the morning of August 13, 1983 and went immediately to an apartment my brother had rented for one month. The plan was for my parents to return home at the end of one month. I would stay and live with Nabil. During that month, Nabil introduced us to the city of Syracuse and the community college I was about to attend in a couple of weeks. OCC sat on top of Onondaga Hill overlooking the city of Syracuse. I had no idea at that time what I was about to face or what the future was holding for me in the US. It felt to me as if I were lost.

Syracuse, New York

During that first month in Syracuse, the four of us—my brother, my parents, and I—spent a significant amount of time sightseeing and getting to know what the city had to offer. Of particular interest to me was my first experience ever in a college setting: Onondaga Community College. My parents were able to visit the college and experience firsthand the environment in which I was to receive my first two years of college education. I was to remain at OCC for two years and then transfer to Syracuse University (SU). Moving from OCC to the larger academic setting of SU would be a gradual process and would make it possible to save my parents thousands of dollars in tuition expenses, since tuition at OCC was much lower than at SU.

Syracuse is a city in Onondaga County. It is the fifth-most-populous city in the state of New York following New York City, Buffalo, Rochester, and Yonkers. The 2020 census showed that the city population was nearly 149,000. Its metropolitan area had a population of nearly 662,000. Syracuse is also well-provided with several convention sites, including a downtown convention complex, and has functioned as a major crossroad for the past two centuries between the Erie Canal and its branch canals, as well as of the railway network. Syracuse is home to Syracuse University, a major research university, as well as Le Moyne College, a nationally recognized liberal arts college. (Syracuse, New York 2021)

After their one-month visit, my parents returned to Palestine, and a few months later, my brother Nabil married his fiancé, Anne, whom he had introduced to my parents during their visit.

My parents remained in Nablus until the outbreak of the first Palestinian Intifada (popular uprising) in 1988. During that year they decided to move permanently to Amman, Jordan.

The Early Months in Syracuse

As soon as my parents returned to Palestine, I moved in with Nabil, his wife Anne, and their two adopted children, Richard and Heather, whose mother, Anne's sister, had been killed in a motor vehicle accident. Richard was a delightful, enthusiastic five-year-old boy who had the mind of a scientist. Heather, Richard's eight-year-old sister, had an outgoing personality and loved to help others.

I remember well the two-bedroom apartment with its tiny living room where we lived. I shared a bedroom with Richard while Heather slept in the living room. Nabil and Anne had their own bedroom. The address was B-1, Apt. 1, Slocum Heights, a Syracuse University housing complex for married students 1.5 miles from the main campus of the University. Skytop, an adjacent housing complex, was for single students. A bus shuttle transported students back and forth to and from the main campus. Three months after I moved in with Nabil and his family, Anne convinced University Housing to allow us to move into a three-bedroom apartment on Chinook Drive in Skytop, even though it was for single students, and due to the small size apartment, we were all cramped in at Slocum Heights. Anne was able to arrange for my first electric wheelchair through the Muscular Dystrophy Association, a private organization. For a couple of weeks, I was relying on a manual wheelchair while going to classes at OCC. With the arrival of this new and wonderful (and fun!) wheelchair, I felt a big part of my freedom had finally arrived! I no longer had to rely on someone else to push my wheelchair. Freedom at last! Freedom at last!

The weather during my first summer in Syracuse was delightful, although at times it was hot, but when winter came, the story was much different. Syracuse gets on average 108 inches of snow each year. It was during that first winter that I experienced firsthand what it was like to drive an electric wheelchair through literally feet of snow. I have experienced my own way of skating on ice as well as getting stuck in piles of snow as the chair's wheels were constantly spinning. At times, I was having real fun, but during other times I had to wait for a passerby to lend a helping hand to free me and my wheelchair from the predicaments of getting stuck. Fortunately, the University kept the pathways and sidewalks clear of snow as much as the weather permitted, and excessive amounts of salt were used to melt the snow to keep the streets passable. Nabil, at the time, was driving an old and rusted station wagon clunker, a 1967 Chevy Barracuda, with a rusted floor, through which I could see the street beneath his car.

I spent the first few months in Syracuse trying to learn as much as possible about life with a physical disability. Verbal communication was difficult. Although I had learned and excelled in English while a student in Palestine, the American accent was not easy for me to understand or imitate.

Chapter Two: My Journey to America 51

Nabil introduced me to Michael Peluso, a quadriplegic student who graduated from SU in 1983. Michael was from Brooklyn, New York, and he became a leading member of an independent living center in Syracuse known as ARISE. After I met Michael, I was invited by him to participate in the center's activities, including workshops that dealt with self-esteem, motivation, activism, independence, personhood, human sexuality, education, laws related to disability, family formation, coping, and many other topics that pertained to the life of people with disabilities. I was indeed fortunate to take part in those activities, and I learned more than I could have imagined in a very short time.

It was during that same year that ARISE led efforts by disabled activists in Syracuse to bring attention to the plight of wheelchair users and their accessibility to transportation. Michael sadly died in 2017 at the age of 60.

Like a fearless soldier, Michael controlled the adversity of his life with courage, skill, and tenacity, successfully completing years of difficult rehabilitation after a motor vehicle accident while at SU.

Michael was a passionate advocate for the disabled. By the time of his death, he had become a Senior Manager with the New York State Education Department (NYSED) where he supervised thirty independent living centers throughout the state of New York. He also acted as NYSED's liaison to the New York State Rehabilitation Council and was an Interagency, Legislative, and Community Relations Coordinator. [He] was instrumental in the reauthorization of the Rehabilitation Act in 1992, testifying before the U.S. House of Representatives Select Committee on Special Education on behalf of the National Association of Protection and Advocacy Systems. He engaged in extensive lobbying efforts in association with the Ticket to Work and Work Incentives Improvement Act, and the Americans with Disabilities Act. He also directed and participated in lobbying the state Legislature for enhanced community-based supports in the areas of accessible transportation, independent living services, deinstitutionalization, and supported employment. He participated in interagency initiatives, developed position papers, and provided public testimony to advance competitive employment outcomes by state-administered vocational rehabilitation programs. (New York State Independent Living Council, Inc., *Michael Peluso (posthumous)* 2018)

Michael Peluso was without question a superior role model for me. I recall one day when Michael encouraged me to participate in a demonstration in downtown Syracuse to introduce wheelchair lifts on city buses. During those demonstrations, wheelchair users protesting their inability to ride on city buses, shackled themselves to the buses, risking police arrests while screaming "We will ride, we will ride!" I told Michael that I would be happy to participate in the demonstrations but that I was unwilling to shackle myself to a bus! After all, I was living in the US on a student visa, and any arrests could jeopardize my legal status in the country. It was during those demonstrations that I was able to witness the courage and determination of activists who were determined to bring constructive change to their world.

Michael Brennan was another quadriplegic user of an electric wheelchair whom I met during my early months in Syracuse. Michael had his own wheelchair-accessible van and was able to drive while sitting in his wheelchair. His van was equipped with a wheelchair lift and he was able to drive using pneumatic technology. I realized then that science and technology could bring freedom to my life even beyond the use of an electric wheelchair. Unfortunately, my family did not have the financial means to purchase such a vehicle, but my hopes never faded. I was shocked to learn for the very first time that driving a wheelchair-accessible van with all the technologies I needed would cost me tens of thousands of dollars. Unfortunately, I could not qualify for any state funding since, at the time, I was not a US citizen.

On many occasions, I would tell Nabil, Anne, Heather, and Richard about what I had learned during the workshops and my encounters with others, especially with both Michaels. During those many months, my brother spent most of his time working on his master's degree at SU,

Chapter Two: My Journey to America   53

while Anne was working at the Syracuse Development Center. On my days off from OCC, I spent most of my time with Richard and Heather playing video games, practicing more of my English-speaking and communication skills, and, of course, learning how to cope with what seemed to me like mountains of snow, maneuvering my electric wheelchair in subzero temperatures.

The Support Structure

The support I received from Nabil and Anne was unparalleled as I lived with them for nearly two years. During that time, I discovered how important it is for anyone, but especially for someone with a disability, to be supported by family members and close friends. Throughout those two years, I developed new friendships with people from all over the world. Supported by family and friends, I determined to make the most of my limited opportunities and do the best I could do in everything I attempted.

I remember with gratitude the support I received from the Office for Disabled Students at OCC, especially from staff members Patrick Fletcher and Rosemary Ann Kelly, both of whom managed the counseling and support services for disabled students on campus. Over time, new questions emerged for me. Will I be able to graduate with good grades? Will I be able to have a girlfriend? Will I be able to drive a car? Will I ever have my own family? Will I ever become independent? Those and other key questions were buzzing in my head as I was plowing my way through the rocky fields of my new life as a young and inexperienced college student.

Faculty members at OCC were extremely supportive and provided me with a solid academic foundation in every possible way. Professors Browne, Haney, Leonardo, and Levy—all professors of mathematics— are among the names of those who served with absolute dedication. I looked up to them, dreaming that possibly one day I, too, could be a professor just like any one of them. I admired what they were able to do and the way in which they did it. In addition to being great teachers and role models they were also great listeners. Whenever I visited them during office hours, they were curious to learn more about my personal journey and my love for mathematics. Thanks to Professor Browne, I will always remember the value of $\sqrt{3}$ as approximately 1.732 since 1732 is the year during which George Washington was born.

I remember well my first English course at OCC. It was Eng153F (the letter F was a designation for foreign students). I completed the course and received an A. I then moved on to Professor Friedman's English class designated for students who needed additional preparation before they could enroll in freshman English courses designed for traditional graduates from American high schools. After only one week as my teacher, Professor Friedman said to me, "Hani, I don't know why you're in my class, but you need to drop this class and register for English 103" (English Composition), the first course in a sequence of two courses designed for recent American graduates.

Professor Elena Levy was a Jewish professor at OCC and a peace activist. She was a member of "Women in Black," an activist group protesting the Israeli occupation of the West Bank, the Gaza Strip, and the Golan Heights by Israel. It was the first group formed by Israeli women in Jerusalem in 1988.

"Women in Black" is one of several Jewish and Israeli organizations who support the rights of Palestinians by ending Israel's military occupation to the occupied territories (Hurwitz et al., 1992). Their voices are not usually magnified in US media.

Zochrot, "remembering" in Hebrew, is an Israeli NGO "working since 2002 to promote acknowledgement and accountability for the ongoing injustices of the Nakba, the Palestinian catastrophe of 1948, and the reconceptualization of the Return as the imperative redress of the Nakba and a chance for a better life for all the country's inhabitants." Its vision is:

Return of the Palestinian refugees to their country on the basis of acknowledgement and accountability, coupled with a joint Jewish-Palestinian process of restitution founded on the principles of transitional justice. This Return will be a central and essential part of the creation of a multicultural democratic space and a joint and equitable fabric of life for all inhabitants of this country on all levels (from home and neighborhood to state level) and in all sectors (economics, politics, and urban planning, but also education, arts and sports). (Zochrot, Our vision 2014)

Jewish Voice for Peace (JVP) has also played a critical role in advocating for Palestinian human rights here in the US. "JVP is inspired by Jewish tradition to work for a just and lasting peace according to principles of human rights, equality, and international law." (*Jewish Voice for Peace*)

Like JVP, "B'Tselem" — The Israeli Information Center for Human Rights in the Occupied Territories — "strives to end Israel's occupation, recognizing that this is the only way to achieve a future that ensures human rights, democracy, liberty, and equality to all people, Palestinian and Israeli alike, living on the bit of land between the Jordan River and the Mediterranean Sea. Various political routes can bring about this future, and while it is not B'Tselem's role to choose among them, one thing is certain: continued occupation is not an option" (*About B'Tselem*).

When we met for the first time, Elena was happy to know that I grew up in Palestine, and a great friendship developed between us. As a professor of mathematics, Elena spent 20 years teaching students who had severe anxieties about the subject of mathematics. In 1991, she published *Contradictions*, a poetry book. In 2012 she published another poetry book, *Legacies and Heresies with Blessings*.

Years later, OCC became the setting for my PhD dissertation work in the effective teaching and learning of mathematics. The mathematics and science department had been recognized for its effectiveness in teaching mathematics to students at the community college level.

Family, friends, and teachers have supported and encouraged me every step of the way, from my early days in Palestine all the way to New York and then to Georgia. I have, indeed, had the good fortune and the blessing of having them all in my life.

Whether in Palestine or in the US, I have always enjoyed academic life and what it brings to the minds and souls of all who seek an education. Day after day and month after month, I worked hard in every course I took, and I even became a mathematics tutor at OCC and earned some extra money in my first paying job as a student in the US.

I knew it was difficult for my parents to find the money I needed for my college tuition, especially after they had already supported my brother's academic journey as an undergraduate student at SU. Fortunately, however, they owned four acres of land that my father had purchased for future investments upon his return from Saudi Arabia, where he had worked for six years with the Arabian oil company Aramco prior to his marriage to my mother in 1955. I am grateful, more than I can say, for their unfailing encouragement and support.

Marching Forward

In 1985, I graduated from OCC after earning 72 credit hours, 64 of which I was able to transfer to SU, where in August of 1985 I was accepted into the School of Computer and Information Science. During that same period, Nabil completed his master's degree in civil engineering and received his first full-time job offer at a company in Washington, DC.

Chapter Two: My Journey to America   57

With Bruce Haney, Professor of Mathematics, Onondaga Community College commencement ceremony, 1985

For the very first time, I began to live on my own outside the framework of my immediate family. In 1984, prior to my brother's departure to Washington, DC, my father was able to send us the down payment for a van that would be used for transporting me to OCC. Nabil had agreed to make the monthly payments on the van, which he left with me when he and his family moved from Syracuse. Although I could not drive the van, I was able to register it in my name, which meant that it could be driven by any of my friends. Relying on them to drive me to and from different places was both awkward and inconvenient, and I always dreamed that someday I might be able to drive a vehicle myself.

When Nabil and his family moved to Washington, I rented an apartment in the old neighborhood of Slocum Heights. SU housing had agreed to rent me a two-bedroom apartment, and I explained to the University that I would be looking for a roommate to assist me with my physical needs. I was allowed to stay in Slocum Heights in a building that had an apartment with a roll-in shower designed specifically for wheelchair users. B11-Apt. 3, Slocum Heights, became my first address living independently in the US.

The search for a roommate began. My disability at that time was progressing slowly but was not severe enough to require constant aid. I thought that any roommate would be able to assist me for a few minutes in the morning and in the evening. I could manage with transferring back and forth from my wheelchair to the bed, the toilet, or the shower seat. I needed only minor assistance in getting dressed in the morning, and for the most part, that phase in my life was an enjoyable one. For a period of two years, I had roommates from India, Jordan, and Lebanon.

On several occasions, along with my friends, I was able to take road trips venturing out of Syracuse to New York City, Albany, Rochester, Binghamton, Buffalo, Atlantic City, Niagara Falls, and Otisco Lake, where I used to love fishing. The most exciting place, however, was the Salmon River Falls in Oswego County, Upstate New York. There, I witnessed one of the most exciting forms of fishing I had ever seen. I was not able to fish without assistance due to the size of the fish and the effort to wrangle the fish from the river. I'm talking about a fish that might weigh 20-30 pounds! As soon as a fish was hooked on the line, everyone else there would pull their fishing lines out of the water until the one who hooked the fish was able to land the fish to prevent tangling the lines. I have seen fish break the lines or escape due to their fighting tenacity and weight. As soon as we returned to the apartment, we cleaned the fish and either smoked it or cut it into fillets that were frozen for future meals.

Me and my friend Ramadan after a fishing trip at Salmon River Falls

From those early years at Syracuse, I can't help but remember meeting a graduate student at SU from South Africa by the name of Thabo Raphoto. He was majoring in adult education. While being a

Chapter Two: My Journey to America

young student in South Africa, he developed a keen interest in issues of justice and that led to his activism, which attracted the attention of the security services of apartheid South Africa and let to Thabo having to flea his country in 1967 to Botswana, then Tanzania, and on to Kenya. He obtained his undergraduate education at the University of East Africa in Nairobi before coming to the US. Thabo and I would share stories about our experiences in our homelands. After the end of the apartheid system, and after receiving his PhD from SU, Thabo went back to South Africa in 1995 and sadly he passed away in 2012. He was buried in Soweto. I was greatly inspired by his activism to achieve freedom for the people of South Africa.

In 1988 Thabo, an activist on the SU campus and the wider Syracuse community, nominated me to become a member of the Third-World Coalition (TWC). TWC is a subgroup of the American Friends Service Committee, a Quaker organization based in Philadelphia, Pennsylvania. As a new member with a disability, I took the lead of a subcommittee of TWC on disability issues from 1988-1944. The goal of the subcommittee was to address disability issues related to third-world, native, and immigrant communities across the United States.

By 1987, wheelchair public transportation in Syracuse became a gradual reality. I was relying on a service called "Call A Bus" provided by the Syracuse City Transportation Authority for people in wheelchairs who wanted to travel within the county limits. The service required 24-hours advance scheduling, but that was an easy thing to do, given that I could organize and schedule my daily and course activities ahead of time. I relied on that service for two years, and buses connecting Slocum Heights with the main campus eventually were equipped with wheelchair lifts.

Between 1985 and 1987, I realized how important education was for my future as a person with a disability, having witnessed how important it was for people *without* disabilities. I became aware of the qualitative shift in assistive technologies that became available for people with disabilities. I began to cherish the freedom provided for me by a country that was established and flourished because of free will and democratic principles. I became interested in reading about US history, the founding fathers, the Constitution, the system of government, disability history, human and civil rights, and struggles for freedom around the world, especially in Palestine and South Africa. I also began reading about the history of the conflict in Palestine from sources that were not readily available to me while I was living there. I began to discover that freedom was, and remains, an evolutionary and revolutionary concept. I began to fall in love with the country that has given hope to millions of people around the world, including myself. The journey out of a disputed land had turned into a personal journey in a promising land.

I took my education seriously, and while challenging the harsh winters of upstate New York, I met all the academic demands of my undergraduate studies. Sometimes I wheeled my chair from my apartment, down East Colvin Street to Comstock Avenue, and all the way to the main campus. I was able to navigate during light to moderate snowstorms as I made my way along the sidewalks with several inches of snow accumulation. On the way to campus, I often met with faculty members, students, and joggers. Whenever my wheelchair got stuck as the snowfall intensified, there always seemed to be someone there who was willing to help. Professor Molina, an SU philosophy professor, was a regular walker from his home to campus.

During the last two years of my undergraduate career at SU I met with wonderful supportive staff and faculty members who admired and encouraged my determination to succeed. At that time, personal computers were emerging on the market, and they were quite expensive. Faculty and students relied on mainframe computers with terminal stations scattered around the campus. I recall when the computer and information systems department chair offered me a computer terminal and a phone modem to be used from home to minimize my commutes to campus.

While some of my friends were partying and having a good time, I was in my apartment doing my homework, working on my assignments with a great deal of care and determination. Week after week, month after month, semester after semester I focused my attention on my studies, and with the blink of an eye, I was near graduation!

I was extremely happy that I was about to graduate from SU, but I had feelings of apprehension about the next phase of my life. Should I stay in this country, become a citizen, and find a job? Or should I go back to Palestine and deal with the unknown? The political climate in Palestine was worsening year after year. During that time, my brother became a US citizen, which meant that he could petition for me to become a citizen too. A new set of critical questions were emerging in my mind like those that were popping up in my head years before while I was living in Palestine. It's always that next phase in our lives that we must learn how to address!

Inspired and encouraged by my high school mathematics teachers in Palestine and my mathematics professors at OCC and SU, I was able to complete dual undergraduate degrees at SU. The first was a BA in mathematics and the other was a BS in computer and information systems.

My parents came from Palestine to attend the graduation ceremony at Manley Field House, an SU sports arena. That was one of the happiest days in my life. Following the commencement ceremonies, my dad drove us in the van and the whole family celebrated at a steakhouse in Syracuse known as Scotch and Sirloin on Erie Boulevard. I could see my parents' pride and happiness in my achievements and in my ability to succeed.

My overall undergraduate GPA and my grades in mathematics were high enough for me to apply to graduate school. I made that decision to continue my education in a field of study that was fulfilling to both mind and soul.

With my proud parents, Syracuse University, 1987

Driving a Vehicle for the First Time

My parents returned to Palestine, contemplating a move from Nablus to Amman, Jordan due to deteriorating conditions under the Israeli occupation during the Palestinian uprising of 1988.

I am thankful for the memory of two wonderful sisters who lived in Syracuse and were active members of St. Elias Orthodox Church. Selma and Evelyn Abdo took it upon themselves to organize the church fundraiser event that allowed me the ultimate physical freedom of being able to drive for myself. Both Selma and Evelyn were single and living together and were both defenders of the Palestinian struggle for independence and freedom. They were so proud of my achievements that they together made my dream a reality.

During the summer of 1987, St. Elias organized an event during which members of the church raised $6000 to defray the cost of lowering the floor of a minivan and equipping it with the hand controls I would need to be able to drive. Care Concepts, an entrepreneurial engineering company in Phoenix, Arizona, had developed a revolutionary design for lowering minivan floors, allowing users of wheelchairs easy access to the steering wheel. Later that summer, I flew

Chapter Two: My Journey to America 63

to Phoenix with my friend Omar, a graduate student at SU originally from Palestine, and we drove back in my 1988 converted Dodge minivan with all the controls I needed to be able to drive. I did not have my driver's license then, but I had a driving permit which allowed me to sit behind the steering wheel with a passenger beside me who was a licensed driver.

We began our journey back to New York from Arizona and I still recall how ecstatic I was to sit behind the steering wheel for the first time in my life. Yes, for the first time in my life I was driving a motor vehicle. I drove for twelve straight hours crossing one state after another on Interstate 40 heading east and leading to Interstate 81 North to New York State. We drove through Arizona, New Mexico, Texas, Oklahoma, Arkansas, Tennessee, Virginia, West Virginia, Pennsylvania, and New York. The trip took us four days with overnight stops. I remember seeing a road sign on I-40 north of Dallas for Palestine, Texas! As soon as I arrived back in Syracuse, I obtained my driving license with flying colors. A new chapter in my life had begun. I would no longer have to rely on anyone else to drive me around.

The first few years in Syracuse had proven to be enlightening. I was able to engage in social activities such as the Muscular Dystrophy Association's (MDA) telethon designed for collecting donations for people with muscular and neuromuscular diseases throughout the nation and in support of patients and research activities. On several occasions I appeared on local TV stations as the national Telethon led by the late actor and comedian Jerry Lewis was being aired nationwide. I felt obliged to assist in that regard, given that MDA had granted me my first electric wheelchair free of charge. I was also able to access the MDA clinic for routine checkups.

While an undergraduate at Syracuse University, I led the Arab Student Association and the Office for Disabled Students. Both organizations held student activities on campus that involved bringing in speakers to address key political and social events relevant to the Arab world, such as American foreign policy in the Middle East and the lives of people with disabilities living in the United States. Becoming a student leader was another aspect that helped me develop a sense of responsibility toward informed citizenship.

Looking Back

Living six thousand miles away from Palestine, I could not help but look back and compare my life there with living in the US. Scenes of military presence were absent from my new reality in the US. People's attitudes toward the disabled were mostly positive and reassuring during my interactions with people. The system of government and the separation between church and government allowed people to channel their energies toward production and competition in ways that moved society forward. That was my impression then, and it remains my impression today. Living in an open society with multiple freedoms and laws that protect the rights of citizens was completely absent from my past.

Despite the amazing privileges of living in the US, there were times when I felt nostalgic and homesick. I remembered my pet cats and dogs, the one sheep my mother bought early in the spring every year to graze around the house, only to be slaughtered midsummer. Oh, and the chickens that were roaming free in the backyard of my house. I remembered my friends coming over to my house to work on school projects or play marbles. However, I became cynical about humanity when I remembered how the Israeli soldiers were patrolling the streets of Nablus in their military vehicles or on foot, displaying their control and dominance of the native Palestinian population. I was extremely sad when I remembered the days I could not go outside my house because there was no or little accessibility to public places. Sidewalks did not have ramps. Buildings, including schools, were not equipped with elevators.

Recalling memories from my past was a routine exercise. Both good and bad memories impacted my life moving forward. Bad memories made me stronger; good ones made me happier. Out of both bad and good, a sense of optimism was born in me.

I began to compare American and Arab societies in ways I could never have imagined. There were vast differences between the two, and finding meaning, a meaning for my life, became much harder to accomplish. In Palestine, my disability was shadowed by the Israeli occupation and by political reality, as well as by people's attitudes toward the disabled person. In America, however, my disability was followed by numerous possibilities away from military conflict and social pressures. I chose to move forward and explore the horizons before me, aiming as high as I could for a brighter and better future.

The next few years of my life proved to be the most significant, both professionally and personally. My journey as a graduate student at Syracuse University began when I was offered both a graduate scholarship and a graduate assistantship in pursuit of yet another dream.

Chapter Three: Education Despite Disability

Introduction

My academic life began in the Department of Mathematics at Syracuse University in the fall of 1987. Based on my academic achievement at the undergraduate level, the department chair at that time, Professor Lawrence Hardy, offered me both a graduate scholarship and a teaching assistantship in the department.

Syracuse University has earned a reputation of being a major research university. The Mathematics Department was composed of nearly 30 full-time faculty and staff members and nearly half that number of teaching assistants, all in a wide range of specialties within the field of mathematics and mathematics education. The Department offered graduate programs leading to MS and PhD degrees in Mathematics and Mathematics Education.

The graduate scholarship allowed me to take graduate courses with a tuition waiver, while the teaching assistantship allowed me to teach two courses every semester with a stipend that helped defray the cost of living. My monthly stipend was nearly $1200.

Carnegie Hall was one of the oldest buildings on campus and was home for the mathematics department. Luckily, there was a small elevator in the building that allowed me access to the department on the second floor. The third floor housed the Erik Hemmingsen mathematics library, while the first floor held many library collections related to the sciences. Erik Hemmingsen was a faculty member in the department who immigrated from Denmark years ago and held the title of Department Chair from 1971 to 1978. He sadly passed away in 2012.

As an undergraduate student, I had Professor Hemmingsen for a course in the History of Mathematics, and he likely had the highest impact on my appreciation for the field of mathematics. His cheerful personality and the love he had for his students were extraordinary. During office hours, I used to visit him in his office to chat about different topics. On. one occasion, he was curious to know how I was able to manage my wheelchair in deep snow, but his favorite topics were mathematics and carpentry. Fortunately, my student office was nearby. I had finally earned my title as a teaching assistant with an office in the building that I shared with other teaching assistants from the department.

The struggle with my disability continued. By then, and luckily, I was able to drive my minivan and was given access to the parking spot nearest to the building. My life was mainly focused on academics: reading, attending classes, lectures, and symposiums, researching, working on assignments, and, of course, enjoying the intellectual presence of similar minds with a common purpose. There were other teaching assistants from all over the world, including the US, India, Germany, Poland, France, Iran, Nigeria, Pakistan, Russia, Lebanon, and Morocco. A renewed sense of purpose emerged in my life. Wanting to do my best became an essential part of my everyday commitment. The support I received from both faculty and colleagues in the department was unrivaled. During that time, my personal life had also taken a major turn.

The Central Role of Education

Through education, a major force all over the world, we transmit knowledge, and with that knowledge we transform our lives and the world in endless ways. In the late '80s, the computer revolution intensified. Instead of relying on mainframe computing systems, the industry began to introduce into the market affordable personal computers that transformed almost every aspect of our lives, including education. For better or for worse, the world since then has forever changed.

As a person with a disability, I was eating from the fruits of science. I used an electric wheelchair and drove a minivan using a set of pneumatic and electronic hand controls. Whether I might be able to perform essential duties for a future job was of little concern to me at the time. My goal was simply to explore the possibilities lying ahead of me.

In my mind, education was synonymous with freedom, exploration, and a continued search for a better future. As a graduate student, I continued my involvement with various student government organizations on campus as leader of the Disability Advocacy Organization (DAO) and as a member of the Arab Student Association.

As a result of my participation in these organizations, I was involved in various activities that led to my extending invitations to recognized speakers to visit campus and give lectures related to physical disability and the Middle East. Dr. David Hartman, a blind psychologist from Roanoke, Virginia, was invited to give a lecture pertaining to the study of human anatomy by blind people, a topic that was of particular interest to blind students. Syracuse University was the first research institution in the nation to create a dual certification program inclusive of both elementary and special education, a testimony to the commitment that the University had toward diversity and inclusion.

The late Clovis Maksoud, head of the Arab League in the UN at that time, was also invited to give a lecture on Palestine. Riyad Mansour, a Palestinian-American diplomat, who since 2005 had been serving as the permanent observer of Palestine to the United Nations, was also among those who were invited. Through such activities, Syracuse University provided me with ongoing and engaging intellectual platforms.

In 1992, I was awarded the Muscular Dystrophy Association's Personal Achievement Award for Central New York. In 1993, based on academic excellence, campus leadership, and community service, I was honored by being selected as a Chancellor's Student Advisor at Syracuse. Dr. Kenneth Shaw (Buzz) was the Chancellor of the University at that time, succeeding Chancellor Melvin Eggers. While I was a graduate student from 1987-1994, I also served on the American

Friends Service Committee as a Third-World Coalition committee member and a Disability Issues subcommittee member.

Professor Sari Knopp Biklen was a faculty member in the Cultural Foundation program at Syracuse University's School of Education. Dr. Biklen, without a doubt, had the greatest impact on my life as a graduate student and on my career. Her husband, Dr. Douglas Biklen, a faculty member in special education (and later Dean of the school of education at Syracuse University) was a pioneer in facilitated communication for people with autism. They were great admirers of my determination to pursue higher education, and never failed to show their encouragement. From Sari, I learned more about education in general than from anyone else, and specifically about gender issues and the history of the American school. She was a qualitative researcher and an ardent supporter of issues of justice around the world. Early in my PhD program, I enrolled in one of her courses on gender issues. I was the only male in the course, and she was impressed with my courage to enroll in a course that normally only female students would be interested in taking. Her enormous contributions to qualitative research in education earned her national recognition. Dr. Biklen was one of the greatest Jewish scholars in the field of cultural foundations of education that I have ever known. In inspiring ways and through her words of encouragement, she had the greatest influence on my intellectual growth and was one of my most valued mentors throughout my graduate work.

My model for becoming an enthusiastic teacher was Professor Sari Knopp Biklen. She was passionate about the cultural foundations for education and taught her classes on this subject with gusto. She later served as a committee member on my PhD dissertation in mathematics education. Sadly, she passed away in 2014.

Professors David Lissner and Daniel Waterman were also among other Jewish faculty members who inspired and encouraged me throughout my journey as a graduate student.

Encouragement can take on many forms. As an undergraduate and graduate student, I was encouraged by general conversations I had with my professors, by their teaching methods and the enthusiastic approach toward the subject matter they taught. I was also encouraged by their discipline to conduct research in support of their chosen disciplines and the overall scholarship of teaching.

During that time, I could not help but recall my past in Palestine. Israelis were Jews (not counting Palestinians who became Israeli citizens after Israel declared itself a state in 1948), and while I was living under their occupation, their actions were oppressive and dehumanizing. However, my own involvements here in the United States with Jews in general and particularly with my Jewish faculty members at Syracuse University were nothing but liberating and humanizing. Even when we disagreed, we were able to accept one another as equals in humanity. Is it because Judaism was hijacked by political and religious Zionism in the same way that Christianity was hijacked by the Crusaders and Christian fundamentalism, and in the same way that Islam was hijacked by Muslim fanatics—is that why Palestinians today experience what they experience in my native land?

Why is it that religions have far too often claimed to be the sole custodians of the truth, and why do we have extreme interpretations and views of the so-called "words of God," only to violate the human rights of others? Is it because religions worldwide have succumbed to political ambitions and have been baptized in the dogmas of extreme ideologies? While reminiscing has been a daily activity of mine, hope and determination to press forward in life, and as essential components of learning, have been my biggest allies. I felt a pressing need to be in full control to independently develop my own views about my world, the present, and future directions.

As an undergraduate student at SU, I was greatly inspired by Professor Fernando Molina, a philosophy professor who used to walk to campus from his home near Manley Field House, a sports arena not too far from the main campus.

Nearly every morning he'd walk about a mile from his home to his office at the university, and I would sometimes in my electric wheelchair meet up with him on the way there from my apartment in south campus, even as the snow fell heavily during the winter season. Professor Molina and I would discuss topics related to philosophy, religion, disability, and politics.

One snowy day he asked me, "Why do you insist on coming to campus in this damn cold and snowy weather on your wheelchair?" "Because I love skating on the snow with my wheelchair," I replied, laughing. He looked at me with a smile and said, "You Palestinians love life." Then I said to him, "Our love for life stems from our resistance in life." Upon arriving at the university campus and before we parted, he told me, "I learned something new from you, Hani." I asked him, "What did you learn, Professor Molina?" He replied, "To challenge the world while smiling." Inspired by our talks, I decided to enroll in his course on the 'Principles of Psychology by William James.'

James' two main schools of thought were pragmatism (the truth of an idea can never be proven) and functionalism (function of behaviors and their practical value). Pragmatism is rooted in the idea that philosophical topics, such as knowledge, language, meaning, belief, and science, are best understood in terms of their practical use (Ruhl, 2020).

The psychology of James confirmed in a way my own thoughts about religions and the roles they can play in our lives. Religions are best explained in terms of their practical use as witnessed by ordinary people. Sadly, Professor Molina passed away in 2017.

Throughout my work as a student and as a teacher, I have been curious to know and learn more about interdisciplinary aspects of education which have led me to become an active member of a community of knowledge seekers. My identity as a Palestinian and later as a Palestinian American was being complemented by the humanity of others, all others. I began to see education as a philosophy of liberation, for it can and should provide all of us with hope for a better future.

Formal and informal trials in any educational endeavor can and must present us with a sense of optimism as we continue to move forward.

As a teaching assistant, I have taught courses in basic algebra, finite mathematics, precalculus and basic courses in calculus at the introductory undergraduate level. I worked with two thoughtful and caring faculty members who were known for their dedication and commitment to quality undergraduate teaching in the mathematics department. They were professors Jack Graver and Aristide Deleanu. Professor Graver grew up in Cincinnati, Ohio and served as an associate chair for the department. Professor Deleanu grew up in Romania. Together they formed a working bond that promoted high standards for teaching in the department. When I became a teaching assistant, both professors clearly wanted me to succeed as a teacher and as a graduate student and they made sure that I had everything I needed to teach my classes. I relied on an overhead projector and transparencies to write on, replacing the traditional blackboard. Every time I taught a new class and on the first day of classes, I could sense the curiosity of my students as I sat in my wheelchair in front of the classroom of 20 to 30 students who were probably wondering about my life and what had led me to become a teacher.

During that period of my life, I began to witness the competitive nature of American society, including higher education. Capitalism became a worldwide economic structure with its own rules under which an increasing number of societies were operating. I began to wonder about the long-term viability of capitalist societies given the social irregularities and challenges that were emerging because of it. Technology began to impact economics and markets worldwide, and I had to find a suitable place for myself in this competitive and technologically driven world. I simply had no choice but to compete!

The course evaluations of my teaching were assuring. My students' scores on common final exams offered by the department were most encouraging and they all seemed to be enjoying my style of teaching. As a result, I felt confident that students were effectively learning from my teaching style and methods. Teaching, therefore, became an appealing idea for a future career.

From Mathematics to Computer Science

While I was taking graduate courses in mathematics, I was also taking graduate courses in computer science and education. The master's degree in computer science at SU was mainly theoretical and mathematically driven. As I began to think about teaching for a future career, I wondered if a master's degree in computer science followed by another graduate degree in mathematics education might form the ideal combination for becoming an effective teacher in a challenging and competitive world.

Professor Howard Johnson, professor of mathematics education and Dean of the graduate school at that time, finally convinced me to combine the two fields of mathematics education and computer science. Computer-assisted instruction was an emerging concentration within mathematics education. I followed Professor Johnson's advice and I switched my major to computer science. The differences between a master's degree in mathematics and that of computer science were minimal.

My motivation combined with that of my professors made my daily struggles much easier to deal and cope with. I was getting physically weaker, but mentally and spiritually I was getting stouter. I was living a battle between the mind and the body, but I was determined to win that battle. The weakening body was making me think with more resolve about a future that remained full of unknowns. I had to do it all and do it by myself.

In the fall of 1988, one of my roommates moved out of the apartment at Slocum Heights. Shortly thereafter I posted two flyers on bulletin boards across the campus. In one of them I announced that I was looking for a new roommate. In the other, I offered my services as a babysitter. I was a little concerned about not being able to find a roommate rather quickly and getting stuck with paying the rent by myself. After all, I was living in the family section of university housing. Two weeks later, I received a call from a young lady in her late 20s who showed interest in my babysitting offer. Her name was Diane.

Diane was going through a divorce and was looking for a babysitter for her two children: Danielle, age 7, and Roy, age 4. After her separation from her husband, she began working at Syracuse Developmental Center and was in urgent need of help with her children. After I was interviewed by Diane, I agreed to babysit for her on the days I was free of other obligations. Given the age of the children and my physical ability at that time, I felt that I could handle both children for a few hours on any given day. A new friendship was in the making and was slowly turning into a love story in a period of two years. In the meantime, I found a roommate who was a post-doctoral student from India. In 1989, Diane's divorce was finalized, and we moved in to live together. Diane and I got married on April 21, 1990, at St. Elias Antiochian Orthodox Church in Syracuse, New York.

With my wife Diane, 1990

Continuing My Journey in Education as a Married Man

I must clearly state that Diane's commitment to me personally and to support my interest in pursuing a PhD degree in mathematics education was clear throughout our relationship and continued through our marriage. My disability was not a factor in her selection of a soulmate. I found her to be a caring and genuine human being who was ready to take on life with me and to fight off its battles. Her resilience and strength have made it possible for both of us to enjoy over thirty years of marriage. Together, we were determined to go share our lives with absolute courage and determination. I began my fatherly duties in my mid-20s as a stepdad.

Diane never saw my disability as an obstacle in any way. Her love was unconditional, and her support was extraordinary. Together we formed a loving family.

I completed my master's degree in computer science in 1989 and I began my course work toward a PhD in mathematics education. The PhD program at Syracuse consisted of sixty graduate semester hours of coursework beyond the master's degree, followed by a dissertation. During that time, I was able to hold both my teaching scholarship and assistantship in the mathematics department.

My coursework consisted of a combination of mathematics and education courses, including methods courses related to mathematics teaching and learning. I began to explore ways to apply qualitative and quantitative research methods and phenomenology applicable to mathematics classrooms. I was especially interested in exploring students' perspectives and attitudes toward mathematics within various cultural contexts. I began reading in areas of cognition, epistemology, and social theory in search of innovative methods for teaching mathematics. Developing and implementing alternative assessment methods in mathematics education was another interest of mine.

Applying technology in the mathematics classroom was at the forefront of innovations in teaching in the department. Professor David Lissner wrote one of the first manuals on how to incorporate graphing calculators into the mathematics classroom at the university. The TI-81 graphing calculator was introduced by Texas Instruments during the late 80s, revolutionizing thereby mathematics teaching and learning for years and perhaps for decades to come. With a background in computer science, I also became involved in teaching with technology.

In the fall of 1992, Syracuse University invited one of the most innovative and emerging minds in mathematics education to join the program. Professor Joanna Osborne Masingila was hired by the College of Arts and Sciences in conjunction with the School of Education and played a significant role in the development of the mathematics education program at Syracuse University. She received her PhD from Indiana University, and her dissertation *Mathematics Practice and Apprenticeship in Carpet Laying: Suggestions for Mathematics Education* appealed to many in the field of mathematics education. Joanna's enormous record of teaching, service, scholarship, and dedication to the field of education culminated with her becoming Dean of the School of Education at Syracuse University.

As soon as Dr. Masingila joined the faculty, the mathematics education program at Syracuse University took off like never before! Joanna had a very strong cross-disciplinary approach to research in mathematics education. I was not the only one rejoicing in her appointment to the department. Joanna's research background and educational philosophy appealed to several graduate students and made her the best choice to lead my dissertation committee.

My PhD Dissertation

Having accumulated 51 graduate semester hours in computer science and mathematics, and 42 graduate semester hours in education, including educational research, I was ready to take on my PhD dissertation in mathematics education.

I must admit that the influence of Dr. Biklen, a well-recognized expert in qualitative research in education, made me contemplate the benefits of qualitative methodology for my dissertation. She is the co-author of *Qualitative Research for Education: An Introduction to Theories and Methods*.

I may have crossed the line as a graduate student grounded in quantitative reasoning by choosing to carry out a detailed qualitative dissertation, but I was glad to do so. Almost my entire background was grounded in quantitative and mathematical reasoning. Qualitative methodology was new to me, and I had to take several graduate courses in educational research and the cultural foundations of education for me to make that shift.

Dr. Biklen guided me through the process of learning about qualitative research with its multiple components: case studies, developing research questions, data collection and analysis (Bogdan & Biklen, 2007), ethnography, phenomenology, and constructivism.

In developing and carrying out my dissertation study, I relied on four theoretical frameworks. They are: (a) the phenomenological approach as it relates to the understanding of events and actions in the classroom; (b) the cultural or ethnographic approach as it relates to students' knowledge, ways of interpreting their experiences with mathematics as a subject, and certainly the influence of their social and economic experiences on their commitment to doing mathematics; (c) the constructivist approach of transforming and negotiating external knowledge about the meaning of doing mathematics and how it relates to defining philosophies and personal views about the self—the process of forming a perspective; and (d) the case-study approach to research in education as it strongly relates to the methodological aspects of this project.

My dissertation committee consisted of Professors Masingila, Graver, and Biklen— Dr. Masingila, with a background in mathematics education, Dr. Graver, with a background in mathematics, and Dr.

Biklen, with a background in the cultural foundations of education. Dr. Masingila served as chair of the committee. I was extremely happy to have the support of all three members throughout the writing of my dissertation, which lasted nearly two years.

In my dissertation, titled *Exploring Perspectives About Mathematics Within the Cultural Context of a College Algebra Class at a Community College*, I wanted to build on a 1991 study by Stage and Kloosterman at Indiana University who explored the existing relationships between ability, beliefs about mathematics, and achievement in introductory college mathematics classrooms. My intention was (a) to determine students' perspectives about mathematics and about themselves as learners and doers of mathematics, (b) to show how these perspectives developed in relation to students' social and cultural backgrounds, and (c) to demonstrate how students continued to develop and change in relation to the social context of the classroom. I also aimed at understanding how teachers used the classroom context and the context of algebra problems to address various issues that students perceived to be influential during their study of algebra.

Data collection included both participant observation and student/teacher interviews. Six algebra students of differing ethnic backgrounds and genders, along with their teacher, were selected from two different sections of the same mathematics course as focus students in this study. These students were interviewed to understand better their (a) cultural and social background, (b) their previous and present encounters with mathematics as a subject and their understanding of the rigors and demands of studying mathematics, (c) their perspectives about the social context of the classroom, and (d) their perceptions of their mathematics teacher. The teacher emerged as a main participant in this study because students looked up to her as a mentor whose partnership and teaching methods included the connection between students' issues and teaching mathematics politically. That teacher was Elena Levy, the 53-year-old Professor from Onondaga Community College.

Professor Levy's political outlook on students' issues connected her to their academic needs, and she was determined to help her students negotiate more realistic meanings for the learning of mathematics. Having taught mathematics for many years, gaining recognition from both colleagues and students, she attempted to consider students' perspectives in her teaching approach.

As a testimony to her many activities in the community, Professor Levy was recognized and honored with several awards. She has published her own books of poetry, which highlight the political, social, and personal struggles people face in the United States and around the world. She has held local photo exhibits from her trips to developing countries.

Professor Levy's outlook on teaching and learning mathematics were like mine. As a teaching assistant, I wanted my students to perceive me as a supporter as well as a mentor who shared with them not only mathematical ideas, but also ideas about the world and other cultures. I wanted to be able to explain to them how cultures define and perceive the world they live in, and how they make sense of their daily living. By doing that, I aspired to diminish the separation between mathematics and the real world in which students lived. I also wanted students to know how the study of mathematics can be inspired by political and social struggles. I have always believed in the diversity of thinking as well as the cultural diversity that exists in this world. Mellin-Olsen (2002) noted that "knowledge does not exist in people in their world, but with people with their world."

The unique relationship between any teacher and the students makes any investigation worth the effort, especially when the investigation helps students create new knowledge and challenge their mind-sets or misconceptions about mathematics and about themselves as learners and doers of mathematics. I am a firm believer in the significance of selecting mathematics teachers based on their reputation among students and based on the teacher's willingness to work with students in and outside the classroom.

My study demonstrated that unless teachers become aware of and consider at every phase of their pedagogy the personal, social, cultural, familial, and institutional issues that exist among their students, what happens in the mathematics classroom may well have little or no significance to students.

Syracuse University, with its faculty and staff members, has given me the opportunity of a lifetime. My dedication finally paid off. I worked diligently to achieve the American dream, my dream, in my new country, the United States of America, along with my American wife, Diane. How thankful I am today for all the memories of the wonderful people I worked with during those years at Syracuse University, which continues to enjoy the reputation of extraordinary academics, distinctive offerings, and an undeniable spirit of commitment to excellence in all its forms. From my experience at Syracuse, I have acquired an honest appreciation for educational and professional diversity at its best.

In his inaugural address as President of Wesleyan University, William F. Chace has said it all:

Generally understood and embraced, diversity is not casual liberal tolerance of anything and everything not yourself. It is not polite accommodation. Instead, diversity is, in action, the sometimes-painful awareness that other people, other races, other voices, other habits of mind, have as much integrity of being, as much claim upon the world, as you do. No one has an obligation greater than your own to change, or yield, or to assimilate into the mass. The irreconcilable is as much a part of social life as the congenial. Being strong in life is being strong amid differences while accepting the fact that your own self can be a considerable imposition upon everyone you meet. I urge you to consider your own oddity before you are troubled or offended by that of others. And I urge you, amid all the differences present to the eye and mind, to reach out and create the bonds that will sustain the commonwealth that will protect us all. We are meant to be here together. (William M. Chace, "The

Language of Action", *The Wesleyan University Alumnus* LXXII, issue number 2, Fall 1989, p. 36)

As I was approaching the end of my dissertation, I began to look for a full-time position as a faculty member either at a community college or at a university. I began to send off applications to colleges and universities across the nation. I had four face-to-face interviews in the States of New York, Oregon, Illinois, and Georgia. I flew to an interview in Oregon all by myself and drove to all others with friends of mine. I still remember the superb view as the plane flew between Mounts Hood and St. Helen, covered in snow, before landing in Portland, Oregon.

During the academic year 1993-'94, I served as an academic advisor at University College of Syracuse University. I was determined to continue my career in a setting like that of University College. After all, my dissertation focused on students' attitudes toward mathematics in a community college setting, so finding a teaching career with nontraditional learners was among my priorities. It was the legacy of Elena Levy that made it possible for me to work with students who had serious apprehensions about mathematics. The next phase of my journey took me from University College of Syracuse University to University College of Mercer University.

My interview in the Deep South was the most fruitful of all four. During the early days of April 1994, I received a phone call from Professor Duane Davis, Professor of Philosophy and Religion at Mercer University. Professor Davis chaired the search committee for a teaching position in mathematics at the rank of Assistant Professor. I was really encouraged at the end of that phone call/interview. A few days later, I received a second phone call from Dr. Davis. The second call was about the decision the committee had made, which was to invite me for a face-to-face interview. That interview took place on April 15, 1994, at the former Tift College campus in Forsyth, Georgia, the home then of Mercer's University College, 65 miles south of Atlanta.

My Journey at Mercer University

On April 13, 1994, my wife Diane, my two stepchildren Danielle and Roy, and I left Syracuse for the anticipated interview at Mercer University. We drove to Washington DC for nearly eight hours and stayed overnight at my brother's home. My brother settled in the DC area after graduating from SU and worked there as a civil engineer. The very next day we continued our drive south toward Atlanta for eight more hours.

On the morning of April 15, at the Hampton Inn in Forsyth, I met with one of the most incredible souls I have ever encountered. That day my whole family met with Dr. Davis as he was waiting for us in the reception area in the hotel. After our introductions, I noticed a box of strawberries in his hands that he invited us to eat from. Throughout the years, Duane became like a second father to me, and our friendship continues until today.

Together we drove to the campus of what had been Tift College two miles away to meet other members of the search committee and the Dean of the College, Professor Joanna Watson. I spent an entire day learning about expectations and the environment surrounding my teaching and work responsibilities should I receive the job offer. I even gave a teaching presentation from my wheelchair using an overhead projector, and my audience consisted of members of the search committee and the Dean.

After meeting with the Dean and members of the search committee, individually and as a group, I was briefed by Dr. Davis about the need for me to be able to drive to multiple remote campuses scattered between the Metro Atlanta area and Macon, a span of nearly 100 miles. I explained that driving was a dream of mine at one point, and I wouldn't mind doing that if I got the job offer. I was also briefed about the profile of the nontraditional adult learners that I would be serving and how my philosophy of teaching would translate into an effective practice in the classroom.

Dr. Davis and I shared lots of memories about our own lives. I was extremely excited to know that Duane and his wife, Mary, were yards away from my high school, Qadri Tuqan, just two years before in a visit to the biblical site of Jacob's well in the city of Nablus.

Jacob's Well is situated inside this Eastern Orthodox church and monastery, Nablus, Palestine (courtesy of Mr. Ameen Abuwarda, Journalist, Nablus)

Duane was not a stranger to the history of that part of the world. His academic background in philosophy and religion speaks clearly about his deep knowledge in theological and historical questions. Duane earned an undergraduate degree in English and Religion from Baylor University in Waco, Texas, followed by four years at the Southern Baptist Theological Seminary in Louisville Kentucky. He received his PhD from Emory University focusing on Christian church history in 1973. He retired from Mercer University in 2008 after a service of nearly 35 years.

The long day of my interview ended with a statement I will never forget. Duane said: "We have another interview for this position, and if I don't see you again, I am so thankful that our paths have crossed." We then said "goodbye."

The next day, we headed back to Syracuse, stopping on the way in Washington DC. One week later, I received a call from Dr. Davis inviting me to join the faculty at Mercer University. Of the 28 years I have been teaching at Mercer thus far, I worked closely with Duane for

15 years prior to his retirement. During those years I had the privilege of working with one of the most spirited and caring souls I have ever known. Duane turned from being a colleague to becoming a true friend and a father figure. To that beautiful mind and gentle soul, I say now, "Thank you from the bottom of my heart for believing in me. Your endless support and guidance made my journey in life not only possible, but so much more meaningful. You and many other colleagues at Mercer University made it possible for me to join a community of truth seekers. How fortunate and privileged I was to be a member of that community for many years."

In August of 1994 I became a member of the faculty at Mercer University. I was not yet finished with my dissertation work. I still had one more chapter to write before my defense. While working at Mercer as a new faculty member I managed to find the extra time to complete my work. In November of 1995, I flew back to Syracuse by myself during a major snowstorm. I arrived at Syracuse early in the morning amid the storm and stayed at the Sheraton Hotel on campus. The next day at around 10 a.m., I maneuvered through the snowy sidewalks from the hotel all the way to the mathematics department in Carnegie Hall, about 1000 yards away. I entered a conference room and greeted everyone. For nearly one hour, I was involved in a Q&A session with my dissertation committee members and invited readers of my dissertation. With absolute confidence, I was able to answer all their questions. I was then asked to leave the conference room for the committee's deliberations. Fifteen minutes later, Professor Deleano, one of the readers and a faculty member in the department, came out and said, "Congratulations, Dr. Khoury!"

I was invited back into the conference room and was congratulated by those who were present. Shortly after, I called my wife Diane and said: "I love you. Dr. Khoury is coming home." After a one-hour celebration by members of the department, I arranged for transportation to the airport, and I flew back to Atlanta that same afternoon.

In 2000, I was promoted to the rank of Associate Professor, and I continued to serve in various administrative roles. During that year I wrote *The Sociological Dimension to Algebraic Instruction: An Interdisciplinary Examination*, a paper that was accepted for presentation at the 3rd International Conference on Creative Teaching sponsored by The World Association for Case Method Research & Application in Lucerne, Switzerland. During my first six years at Mercer, I focused primarily on my teaching, curriculum design, basic research focusing on the scholarship of teaching, and on service to the University and the community at large. In 2008, I was promoted to the rank of Professor.

My Interest in the Middle East while Teaching at Mercer

While at Mercer University, I continued my active involvement in academic topics related to the Middle East and disability. I wrote several articles in the Macon Telegraph about Palestine and US foreign policy in the Middle East vis-à-vis the Palestinian search for independence. My articles drew attention from community members. Only then did I discover the huge impact the politics of the Judeo-Christian tradition had on the minds of people in the United States, especially in the South. For many, the creation of Israel was in fulfillment of Holy Scripture according to the Old Testament, and the blessings of God would only be extended to those who bless Israel. Israel's treatment of the Palestinian people was totally ignored by them, if not justified as fulfillment of scripture.

In 1996, the chairman of the Palestine Liberation Organization, Yasser Arafat, visited President Carter in his hometown of Plains, Georgia, also the President's birth city, one hour south of Macon. Chairman Arafat wanted to extend a personal "thank you" to President Carter for observing the first Palestinian legislative and presidential election in the West Bank and the Gaza Strip. I had the privilege of meeting Chairman Arafat briefly during that visit. President Carter presented Chairman Arafat with the key to the city of Plains in appreciation for his peace efforts.

86   Giving Up Is Not An Option

Palestinian leader Yasser Arafat during 1996 visit to Plains, GA
Background shows President Jimmy Carter

Yasser Arafat was the Chairman of the PLO from 1969-2004 and the President of the Palestinian National Authority (PNA) from 1994-2004. He led the Fatah political party (1959-2004) which was founded under the desire to free Palestine. Arafat died in 2004 from a mysterious blood disorder. Several theories surrounded his death and among them was poisoning by a radioactive material placed into a meal he had eaten hours before showing symptoms of illness.

Israel and/or political rivals of Arafat within the Palestinian Authority were among those who were accused in the alleged assassination.

In 2000, I invited Jewish theologian Marc Ellis to speak at Mercer University. I have always been an admirer of Jewish liberation theology. In one of his presentations, Professor Ellis said:

I have wrestled with the challenges to Jewish identity and ethics that confront us through the Holocaust, anti-Semitism, ecumenism, and the Israeli-Palestinian conflict. During this time, a Constantinian Judaism has emerged, Israeli expansionism has continued, progressive Jews have faltered, and an exilic community comprised of Jews of conscience has evolved. Anti-Semitism has been on the rise. This new century presents us with an opportunity to choose the future of Jewish life that is characterized by an honest reckoning and compassionate action worthy of the Jewish ethical tradition. The time, though, is late, and the road ahead rife with complexity and divisiveness. Is there a way forward? Will such a path precipitate a break with a Jewish tradition defined by mainstream Jewish institutions and the academic classifications of Holocaust and Judaic Studies? Can we enter on a path that deepens Jewish particularity while also emphasizing Jewish universality? (Ellis, 2000)

With Jewish Theologian Marc Ellis during his visit to Mercer University and Georgia College and State University, 2000

In 1998, I served as a member of the Macon Council on World Affairs and Director of the Mayor's Commission on Disability Issues in Macon. During that year, I invited the late US Representative Paul Findlay from Illinois to give a lecture at the University on US foreign policy in the Middle East. Following the lecture as I was driving him to the airport, I shared with him some of my thoughts on the relationship between teaching, politics, and honest citizenship. On the way, Mr. Findlay mentioned the name of a retired British mathematics professor by the name of Colin Hannaford, director of the Institute for Democracy from Mathematics in England.

He promised to provide me with Professor Hannaford's contact information as soon as he returned to his office. He did indeed, and a new friendship was forged with yet another fascinating mind.

Professor Hannaford believed in the moral and social implications of mathematics teaching. He was advocating for teaching mathematics as Socrates intended: to cultivate people's active, self-critical, co-operative intelligence. He served as chair of Mathematics and Ethics in several European Schools up until 2004. Before that, he had served in the Royal Military Academy in Sandhurst, England.

My Journey with Colin Hannaford

After being awarded tenure in 2000, I began to invest a considerable amount of time working with Professor Hannaford on promoting what we both believed to be crucial in achieving constructive actions in the world, beginning in the classroom. We both believed that the world was in danger and that education worldwide was not doing enough to achieve that goal.

In 2005, I invited Professor Hannaford to visit Mercer University, where he gave two lectures on the moral and social implications of mathematics teaching. We both perceived mathematics not only as one of the best "exemplifiers" of analytical and critical thinking, but also of honest citizenship. We began to warn against a decline in mathematics education which will most likely lead to a decline in democratic thinking. A decline in democratic thinking could always lead to fracturing societies. We asked, "What is of universal benefit to humanity?" The answer, we suggested, was the powerful inclination to be honest with ourselves and with others. This innate morality, however, may be virtually destroyed by the demands of a competitive education and the demands it puts on students. Morality, we believed, would survive only as the creative impulse of mathematical reasoning.

After my promotion in 2008, I continued to work with Professor Hannaford on possible ways to promote our ideas. Together, we served as members of a task force organizing a series of international conferences and forums sponsored by the Qatar Foundation in Doha, Qatar and by UNESCO. We traveled to both Qatar and Jordan to promote those ideas. The goal of these conferences was to offer a forum for international scholars to explore the implications of their research for practical educational applications. The series began in 2004 with a forum dedicated to the Arts and Sciences Partnership, and in 2006 the focus shifted to the exploration of Technology, Empowerment, and Education.

With Aljazeera news anchor, Fairouz Ziani, Doha, Qatar, 2006

In 2009 I wrote a paper titled *Citizenship and Mathematics: The Importance of Dialogue in Mathematics Teaching and Learning*. It was selected for presentation at the 20th Annual International Conference on College Teaching and Learning held in Jacksonville, Florida and was one of a small number of papers selected for publication in the conference's "Selected Papers." It addressed the importance of discussion in mathematics and science education as related to culture and citizenship in the United States and internationally.

The paper argued for the development of a genuine understanding of citizenship through the exploration of mathematics and science. Higher education must be held responsible for developing policies and strategies aimed at helping communities develop perspectives that would either reinvent or rejuvenate traditions that recognize the importance of mathematical and scientific proficiency, but why?

It's because democratic societies have a lot to risk if the roles of evidence and dialogue/intellectual leadership vanish from the spheres of public debate and popular culture.

Mathematics and science classrooms can help us develop and maintain a genuine understanding of democratic thinking and informed citizenship. There are parallels between the pedagogical evidence and the social evidence to be made. According to my colleague Colin Hannaford, Director of the Institute for Democracy from Mathematics in England, there are three axioms for the social evidence of democratic thinking. They are:

1. Leaders' policies are only finally confirmed as satisfactory by the people's free understanding and assent.
2. Political leaders must treat their people — and they must learn to treat each other — as political equals.
3. All the leaders' policies must be openly and completely explained.

The above axioms could be easily introduced in mathematics classrooms as the pedagogy can parallel that of the social evidence.

1. Mathematical arguments are finally confirmed as satisfactory only by students' free understanding and assent.
2. Teachers must treat their students, and the students must learn to treat each other, as intellectual equals.
3. All the teacher's arguments must be openly and completely explained.

During the same year, I gave a videotaped presentation titled Climates in the Mathematics Classroom in an international conference on "Using Mathematics Education in Schools to Give Peace a Voice". The conference was held at St George's House, Windsor Castle, and focused on encouraging classroom cultures and climates that promote democratic behaviors as the means to fostering inter-cultural and inter-faith understanding and tolerance. Arranged by Professor Hannaford, the conference was attended by educators from France, Germany, Hungary, Jordan, United Kingdom, United States, and Qatar. In 2010, Colin and I traveled to Amman, Jordan for a presentation at the Arab Thought Forum, focusing on promoting classroom climates conducive to the principles of democracy and citizenship.

Chapter Four: Embracing a Nation and a Family

Introduction

Citizenship has many significant dimensions. It provides for a sense of belonging to multiple frameworks within our lives. It is linked to country and national identity as well as to value systems. I became a citizen of the United States in 1994, but that did not make me a citizen in the fullest sense. Citizenship is also what you give to others. It is what you do for and with fellow human beings who are residing within your space, and without its being honest, it is destined most likely to fail.

Years after living in this landscape of dreams we call America, I felt it was time for me to "give back" in any possible way to society and to the country that was willing to accept me as one of its own.

Being a citizen of the United States of America has given me not only a sense of equality under the law as a person with a disability, but also a set of values and ideals that have shaped the person I am today. Freedom, liberty, opportunity, and employment within a functioning economy are among the many things I have enjoyed as a citizen of my newly embraced country. Assimilating into this melting pot of people from all over the world took an incredible amount of hard work, but in the end, the makeup of American society made it possible for me to function independently and become a productive member of society.

In 1994, and shortly after I moved to Georgia from New York, my family and I were welcomed by both Mercer University and the larger community. I felt the warmth and hospitality of people in the south.

Given the demands of driving for my new teaching responsibilities, the Georgia State Department of Rehabilitation was extremely supportive of my new endeavor as a faculty member at Mercer. The Department paid for a new set of adaptive equipment that I needed to

Chapter Four: Embracing a Nation and a Family

drive a new vehicle. In 1995, I said goodbye to my rusty 1988 Dodge Caravan after enduring years of salty roads in the harsh winters of New York.

Both Danielle and Roy attended public schools in Macon. In 1998, Danielle graduated from high school and attended Mercer University for a degree in Liberal Studies and graduated in 2002. Roy, on the other hand, after graduating from high school, took a few courses at a local technical college and then joined the workforce.

A few years later, both Danielle and Roy married, had children of their own, and began to pave their own way with their own careers. Shortly after they moved out, both Diane and I felt the empty-nest syndrome. I was spending a substantial amount of my time teaching and traveling between the various academic centers of Mercer University. Mercer offered classes at multiple locations such as the Douglas County Center in Lithia Springs, fifteen miles west of Atlanta, the Griffin Center 35 miles south of Atlanta in the city of Griffin, the Covington Center, 20 miles east of Atlanta in the city of Covington, the Eastman Center, 50 miles southeast of Macon in the city of Eastman, and two additional centers, one on the main campus in Macon and the other on the Atlanta campus.

While I was away from home, Diane spent much of her time reading books and magazines. One day, after reading an article in the local newspaper about the urgent need for foster homes locally and regionally, Diane suggested that we open our home to foster children. Even though we did not have children of our own, the idea of fostering or adopting children had never crossed our minds. We were happy just being able to raise Danielle and Roy. We both felt, however, that we could give back to society in a meaningful way. We welcomed the idea, but one of the most tragic events of my life stood temporarily in the way: the death of my father.

Saying Goodbye to My Father

After spending nearly two decades away from my aging parents, I began to encourage them to relocate with me in the US. Early in 2002, after the tragic incidents of September 11 the previous year, my parents planned for a long-term visit with me and my family in Georgia. At the time, my father was nearly eighty-three years old. Nearly twenty years earlier he and my mom had brought me to Syracuse to continue my educational journey. Their visit with us was not their first trip to Georgia. They had visited us in 1998 but for only one month. The twenty years between my arrival in Syracuse in 1983 and my parents' arrival in Georgia in 2002 went by like the blink of an eye.

Upon their arrival, I was determined to spend as much time as I could with both of my parents, but especially with my dad. His health was deteriorating due to a weakening heart and bleeding intestines. Exactly as I did during their visit in 1998, I was determined to bring my parents along with me to my teaching sites, making my traveling much more enjoyable and memorable. During those hours of driving, we were all reminiscing and pondering the future. In doing so, I was trying to repay part of the huge debt I owed my parents in the form of joyful gratitude. I wanted my parents to feel and witness my enthusiasm and love for teaching. This was only one of the few ways I could say "thank you."

Being in an electric wheelchair did not deter my desire to create nice memories with my father. He couldn't take my hand to lean on it while he walked, but I didn't lose hope. I came up with an idea and made what you see in the picture below — a wooden platform fixed to two wheels and two pieces of steel. It was attached to my wheelchair with two short chains so that I could pull him behind me while he was standing on it! I would like to think he had more fun with it than I did.

Chapter Four: Embracing a Nation and a Family

My father's ride-a-long

My parents had given me throughout the years unconditional love and support, and I was determined to share that gift of caring, not only with my family, but also with my students. Love is a fascinating gift and can be channeled in seemingly endless ways and into unforeseeable futures.

On the way to my teaching sites, we would stop at grocery stands along the way to buy strawberries, muscadines, watermelon, and peaches from the peach capital of the Deep South, but my dad's favorite fruit was undoubtedly those shiny red strawberries.

My father's health was in constant decline. He suffered from severe pain from arthritis and from ongoing bleeding in his large intestine. A tumor was forming on his right kidney, and finally on Christmas Day 2003, my father passed away at the Medical Center of Central Georgia from heart failure. He was buried in Macon Memorial Park Cemetery near my home. On his gravestone are two engravings. The first shows his birthplace in Palestine and the second, a strawberry plant, signifies our joyful memories while traveling together to my various teaching sites. His loss was one of the most saddening experiences in my life.

My father died at the age of eighty-four, but his legacies of love and sacrifice will forever be cherished by many, and especially by me. His marriage to my mother lasted for nearly fifty years, and I promised him that I would care for mom for as long as I could. She has continued to live with Diane and me, and she is about to celebrate her 93rd birthday.

My father at the age of 77

In loving memory of my father Qustandi Nicola Khoury
Macon Memorial Park, Macon, GA, USA

Chapter Four: Embracing a Nation and a Family

Our Foster Home

After the passing of my father, the idea of fostering children resurfaced in 2005. My father's death made me far more determined to give to and care for others as much as I was cared for by my parents. Diane and I began to foster neglected children held by the Department of Family and Children Services (DFACS) in Bibb County in central Georgia.

To be certified by the State of Georgia as foster parents, we had to take classes offered by DFACS for eight consecutive weeks and our home had to be inspected for space and safety matters concerning foster children. Background checks and letters of recommendation were sought before we were confirmed as foster parents. Within a few months, our home was opened to help the most vulnerable in any society: children.

Living in Palestine under the Israeli occupation and having a disability of my own were extremely difficult challenges that I had to endure and cope with earlier in my life, but after encountering the turbulent lives of foster and adopted children who lived with us over the years, it seemed to me that the world was moving, socially speaking, in alarming directions. Questions concerning justice and fairness reappeared, but this time in a totally different context. It was not only a question of my own disability or the political climate under which I was living. I also began to ask questions concerning the suffering and plight of neglected children in one of the most powerful nations on earth.

Late in 2005, Diane and I began our fostering journey with two newborn baby girls named Lora and Juli. A few months later, Mark, a seven-year-old boy, arrived at our home. I didn't know at that time the scope of the word "neglected," but after being debriefed by DFACS and getting to know those children firsthand, what came to mind first was their fractured and dysfunctional family structures. (It is important to mention here that all the information and accounts provided herein are factual, while actual names have been changed to protect the identity and maintain the anonymity of all the children.)

Juli's and Lora's birth parents were substance abusers, so the two girls were in the custody of DFACS to protect them from eminent neglect. Mark, on the other hand, was removed from his home due to allegations of emotional abuse.

A few months later, Mark and Juli were reunited with their birth parents. Juli's mom gave up drugs completely, while allegations against Mark's birth parents were unsubstantiated and therefore were dropped. Lora, on the other hand, continued to live with us as our only foster child.

Shortly thereafter, within a couple of months, Ron, a three-year-old boy and one of three siblings living in another foster home, arrived at our home. Ron had been removed from several foster homes due to behavioral problems. Within another couple of months, we agreed to take in Ron's siblings, Cindy (seven years old) and Sami (nine years old), to keep all three children together.

The goal of every DFACS case has been the reunification of every foster child with his or her birth parents. Once a child is in the custody of DFACS, the agency assigns a review panel to determine compliance by the birth parents with a reunification process and plan determined by DFACS and the juvenile legal system. Failure to comply usually leads to the termination of parental rights by a court order. In most cases when parental rights are terminated, foster children will be eligible for adoption. Before getting to that point, however, DFACS will seek immediate or extended family members who would be willing to assume legal guardianship of the foster child. If no qualified family member steps forward to assume guardianship of the minor child, the child will be declared available for adoption, and priority is usually given to foster parents.

Chapter Four: Embracing a Nation and a Family

For two to three years, attempts by the birth parents of all four children (Lora and the three siblings) to reclaim their parental rights were declared hopeless. DFACS gave the birth parents plenty of time to curb habits of substance abuse and to gain employment, but those efforts were completely neglected. In 2008, parental rights to all four children were terminated by a court order and all four of them were declared eligible for legal adoption. None of the children's immediate or extended family members wanted the additional responsibility of caring for any one of them. Several of them were also substance abusers.

One late evening on October 2006 on my way home after teaching one of my classes at one of Mercer's locations, I narrowly escaped death — I would say miraculously — in an automobile accident involving three tractor trailer trucks on a major highway. Fortunately, though my own vehicle was rendered unrepairable, I was unharmed. Escaping this accident was a significant event which led me to make yet another important decision in my life: moving from foster care to adoption. I felt like I was granted an extension on my life.

Diane and I were next in line to be asked if we wanted to adopt all four of them. To that, we said "Yes!"

In the pages that follow, I will narrate the details surrounding the lives of all four of our adopted children from the time they arrived at our home.

Lora's Story:

Lora was a newborn when she arrived at our home. She is African American, and her parents were substance abusers. Her birth mother had previously given up several of her children to legal guardianship or adoption and showed no interest in keeping Lora. Her natural father also showed no interest in keeping Lora. He, too, was unwilling to give up his addictive habits of substance abuse. Lora was my first adoptive infant. When she arrived at our home, she was greeted joyfully by the whole family. At the time of my writing this book, Lora was thirteen years old. Throughout the years that Lora has been in our care, I have learned much about race and race relationships in America. For example, I have learned that transracial adoptions were mainly legalized by the passing of the Multiethnic Placement Act of 1994 and the Adoption and Safe Families Act of 1997. Until 1994, transracial adoptions were viewed as harmful to racial identity! Sadly, the wounds resulting from a long history of racial and other forms of discrimination are deep within American Society,

As Lora grew up, Diane stood by her every day and every night, making sure that her needs were met. While she was an infant, we would put her in a cloth carrier and strap her to our bodies. Shortly after she learned to walk, I would take her with me everywhere I could by allowing her to stand on a platform designed as a footrest attached to my wheelchair. She did that while holding her hands to my knees. Together, we went to shopping malls, grocery stores, playgrounds, amusement parks, and pet stores, and there was nothing like the looks in people's eyes as they stared at us. She even turned out to be an animal lover, just as I am. Cats were our favorite pets. Here I was, a guy in a wheelchair roaming around different places with Lora, who happened to be black. I wish I could know what people were thinking, but I can only guess!

Lora has contributed to my life, and to our lives as a family, in many ways. She was not only an infant when she arrived at our home; she was also a person of color. In that regard, I have felt the blessings and the joy of having her from the beginning of her life, watching her grow up to be a beautiful young black lady. Deep inside, as I watched her grow up, I felt a deep desire to endorse her racial heritage and to encourage her to take pride in and be grateful for the person she is and the person she can become in future years.

When Lora reached the age of five, Diane and I decided to explain to her, to the best of our abilities, the meaning of adoption. Lora had assumed that she came from Diane's belly and that God had painted her

Chapter Four: Embracing a Nation and a Family

brown and that daddy and mommy were painted white. When Lora went to kindergarten, one of her classmates told her that we were not her real parents. She came home upset and at that point we began to explain what adoption was all about. The difficult questions then began to emerge. Lora began to ask Diane, "Did I come from your belly?" and "Why didn't my real parents want to keep me?" and "Were they bad people?" and . . . the list of questions went on and on.

It was difficult for us to explain to her about the ramifications of choices that people make in their lives, although we tried on many occasions. We've assured her that her birth parents were not bad, but that they made some wrong choices. We, as her adoptive parents, could only pledge to her that the love we had for her was unconditional and limitless.

After we adopted Lora in 2008, we allowed her birth family members to visit her at our home if they would keep consistency in their visitations, once a month, once every two months, or any other interval that we could agree on. Unfortunately, that did not happen. Lora grew up knowing that she has birth brothers and sisters, but she was also aware that she had been completely separated from her birth family.

My mother's relationship with Lora was a very special one. She embraced Lora as one of her own grandchildren, having fallen in love with her the moment she arrived at our home. That special bond continued through the years to get stronger and stronger.

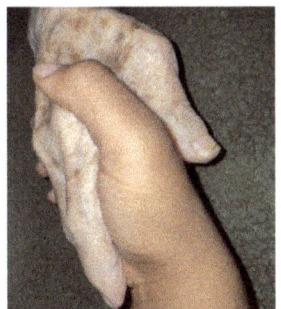

The eternal bond of love between two giant souls: My mother and my daughter

Ron's, Cindy's, and Sami's Stories:

Ron arrived at our home at the age of three, only a few months after Lora's arrival. He was diagnosed at the age of five with ADHD — Attention Deficit/Hyperactivity Disorder. His background was filled with tragedies and misfortunes, given the abandonment he went through as an infant. He entered our foster care after being rejected by another foster-care family.

Diane and I met with Ron and his case worker in hopes of giving him another chance, this time at our home. He was an energetic kid whose mind was racing in all directions. Attention disorder and hyperactivity were difficult for him to control. He was highly intelligent, but his disorder stood in the way as he grew older. Several of his life experiences were traumatic. He and his siblings lived with his maternal grandparents for a while, but their inability to abide by court orders of complete separation from their birth parents forced the court system to move them into foster care, only to be rejected by those foster families.

Ron's behavior later as a teenager was greatly influenced by what he had witnessed as a child. He and his siblings, whom we later adopted, went through horrifying experiences, such as going hungry and being fed by neighbors. The neglect, delinquency, and exposure to improper behaviors by their birth parents and other family members became influential in their lives later as teenagers.

Regardless of all that, Diane and I welcomed them to our home, pledging to do our best as foster parents and later as adoptive parents. I was guided by my beliefs and my own experiences as a child who was never rejected by his own parents or by any other person. Both Diane and I were and remain strong supporters of giving others a second chance, maybe more, to improve the quality of their lives. I believe that it was in me as an educator, and as someone who cherished the value of life and the gifts it brings along with it, to accept the idea of caring for Ron as a child. He was the fourth foster child to arrive at our home.

Chapter Four: Embracing a Nation and a Family

Six months later, Ron's sister Cindy arrived at our home, another child rescued after being rejected at another foster home. Cindy was seven years old with behavioral problems and was later diagnosed with ADD — attention deficit disorder.

Keeping up with doctor appointments, schooling, and school activities, Diane and I found social activities to be incredibly rewarding experiences for us as parents. We were gradually becoming aware, however, of the influence of substance use and neglect on the lives of both Ron and Cindy. Symptoms of reactive detachment and opposition defiance behaviors began to surface as they became teenagers. We received help and counseling, only to be told that it was typical teenage behavior. For Ron and Cindy, behaviors like lying and stealing became alarming and troublesome. The legal age in the State of Georgia when children can leave home without being forced to remain in the custody of their parents is seventeen. At that age, both Ron and Cindy moved out with their birth family, following in the footsteps of their oldest sibling, Sami.

The Department of Family and Children Services (DFACS) had an interest, understandably, in keeping all three siblings together. Sami was not rejected by his previous foster home, but the interest in keeping the three of them together made him join his brother and sister.

For the entire period of nine years, Sami was the most pleasant and mannered child I had ever seen. He was academically inclined but was drawn more toward a different lifestyle. As a child, and as a teenager, Sami was interested in building model cars and riding dirt bikes, reminiscing his days with his birth parents. Unlike his siblings, Sami did not have academic problems or concerns in middle or high school. He was growing up and was ready to take on life in the same way he did when he was trying to provide his siblings with food and protection. Deep inside, he felt that he was responsible for them, even though they were being cared for by us.

The formal adoption of all four children took place in 2008. Sami, being the oldest, had many memories with his birth parents, who could visit him and his siblings at our home under certain rules that we had established: consistency, transparency, and accountability.

One evening, Sami was informed that his birth parental rights had been terminated by a court order. Diane and I as foster parents explained to him that he, along with his siblings, were up for adoption and that none of his extended family members were ready to assume that responsibility. He burst into tears, and we then asked him, "Do you want to be adopted by us?" He emphatically replied, "Yes!"

Diane and I realized, through formal training prior to foster care and adoption, that the love children hold for their birth parents, even when children are being neglected or abused, is, and will always be, unconditional. Maybe it's difficult for some to understand, but on that evening, I could see it in Sami's eyes. At that time, I told Sami that our job as adoptive parents was to help him grow in a safe, loving, and secure environment, under the rules of the household. Sami was emotionally tied to his birth parents, whom we had met on several occasions, even though they were substance abusers. I even assured him that if he chose to live with them after the age of eighteen, it would be his right to do so.

We are not sure as adoptive parents whether the three siblings had been in touch with their birth parents later in their teenage years through the Internet, social media, or e-mail, but most likely, if they had been, they were doing it in secret, even though their birth parents were permitted to visit with them under certain rules established by the judge of Juvenile Family Court. (We are not sure whether pressures were exerted on them to move out at the legal ages of seventeen or eighteen. Such decisions are typical of local adoptions of young children.)

In 2013, Sami, as a high-schooler, and ten students from Mercer University accompanied me on a mission trip to Jordan, where we held a recreational camp for orphaned children in the capital of Amman. A

Chapter Four: Embracing a Nation and a Family

year later, shortly after he celebrated his eighteenth birthday, Sami moved out to live with his father. His mother was still in prison for repeated criminal offenses. His father had remarried and had two stepchildren.

Sami could have gone to college and done well, but he chose not to do so, given the circumstances under which he was living. His unanswered questions had haunted him through the years. He, along with his siblings, were searching for answers to one of the most difficult questions I ever had to grapple with: "Why me?"

Maybe it was time for all three children to re-create the years they had missed as very young children with their birth parents. I'm almost certain that it was on their mind that they could do so, even though it was not possible in those earlier years. None of the three were academically inclined enough to go to college, nor did they see the long-term importance of academics, but they ultimately felt that they were free to choose their own paths.

Freedom is what we all aspire to, and all three siblings were interested in experiencing life in a way they themselves believed they could manage, even at a young age. Attending college free of charge, given that I was working as a faculty member at the university, was never seen by them to be a real and significant opportunity.

There is no doubt in my mind that I have lived, and continue to live, the best part of my life with children I have chosen to adopt. Their stories make me even more determined to continue my journey as a supporter of human rights for all. Children in America deserve a great deal more attention in a country that struggles at times with its own priorities.

Neither Diane nor I believe we have wasted any time helping all three siblings overcome one of life's most devastating experiences at critical ages: being able to comprehend living away from where they truly believe they belong. On the contrary, we believe that the years they spent with us will provide for them an opportunity for thoughtful and serious reflection as they grow older.

The stories you have read here are a constant reminder to me of my own story. Although I have adopted America as my new homeland, my eyes through the years have been looking back toward a free Palestine. Though the eyes fail to see, the heart will not.

The feeling of "belonging" will always remain at the core of searching for our own truths. Some of us are determined to search for answers to our own questions as we contemplate the future, while others are determined to dig into the past as they contemplate the present. Whatever we do, life will persistently unfold in ways that go beyond our own imagination, and certainly beyond our own expectations.

Chapter Five: Mathematics Education and the Future of Democracy — A Professional Perspective

Introduction

In his paper *A Guide to Writing Mathematics*, Kevin Lee (2010) writes, "The Greek word *mathemas*, from which we derive the word 'mathematics,' embodies the notions of knowledge, cognition, understanding, and perception. In the end, mathematics is about ideas" (p. 1).

Mathematics is one of the best examples of not only analytical and critical thinking but also of honest citizenship. Why? Because at the heart of democracy lie two essentials: questioning and debating. Questions and debates are clearly key ingredients of mathematical/analytical reasoning and of critical thinking. It is my belief that a decline in mathematics education will lead to a decline in democratic thinking, and a decline in democratic thinking is an omen of a potential future, a fractured society. If you were to ask me, "What ingrained concept do you believe to be of universal benefit to humanity?" I would answer and affirm without hesitation, "It is the powerful inclination to be honest with ourselves and with others. This kind of honesty is best exemplified in the art of mathematical thinking. This form of innate morality could be destroyed by the demands that a competitive education may put on us all, especially students. Morality can survive only if the creative impulse characteristic of mathematical inquiry survives."

Mathematics is a critical tool for creative and innovative thinking. Practically speaking, it is a powerful means for liberating humanity from its own prejudices. In this chapter, I will share my journey as a mathematics educator and will discuss my own ways of thinking about mathematics and its implications for the other sciences and for the humanities.

Academic Excursions

In both 2006 and 2007, I was invited to Doha, Qatar (a small country east of and bordering Saudi Arabia) to give a presentation at an international conference about the social implications of teaching and learning mathematics through dialogue and contextual analysis of mathematical problem solving. During my presentations, I affirmed that the rate of change (development) in society should be far more significant to policy makers than change itself. Change is willful, dynamic, and central to democratic thinking. Democracies evolve by changing, hopefully constructively.

During my presentation, I acknowledged that there must be time for reflection and response by the society for change not to be artificial. The question remains, "What role does the teaching and learning of mathematics play?"

If you think about mathematics as being helpful in balancing your checkbook, managing your small business, or as a gateway to a world of abstraction, your scope of understanding the potential power of mathematics may be limited. Let's acknowledge, however, that mathematics has been defined by some as a science of patterns and by others as a universal language. Undoubtedly, these are good characterizations of mathematical reasoning, but they are limited in scope when we examine the effect of mathematics on the humanities. My suggestion is to perceive and teach mathematics as a series of arguments. Arguments (debates) are undoubtedly powerful tools to advance meaningful and constructive change within and around us.

A proof, for example, consists of a rational mathematical argument or a series of linked arguments. Similarly, a debate may be characterized as a sequence of factual responses of opposing views within society. Proofs and debates utilize the learned method of critical thinking.

Combined with the effective use of language and communication skills, mathematical arguments mimic debates within a society. Mathematics, taught as a series of arguments, and social debates within the society are transformative tools that can help us connect not only with mathematics as a body of mathematical content, but also with mathematics as a formal exchange of ideas (dialogue) seeking to advance knowledge and to reach a consensus.

Through debate — a healthy dialogue or exchange of ideas from different or opposing views within groups of people — we can build and/or advance democratic societies. Debates/mathematics, taught and learned as a series of arguments, have the potential for developing habits of mind that may transform the mind itself and all society through the diversity of thought.

The Relationship between Mathematics and Reasoning for Democracy

According to my colleague Colin Hannaford, Director of the Institute for Democracy from Mathematics in Oxford, England, "The original purpose of mathematics teaching is unknown to all but a handful of classical historians. They know that the style of argument on which mathematics depends was always intended to give more political freedom to ordinary people, to increase their confidence in democracy. Its purpose is to persuade people to accept logical truths freely and voluntarily, not to be bullied or oppressed by dogma or dogmatists to accept their ideas as absolute truths."

Do we ever solve a mathematics problem and witness certain habits of mind concerning freedom, justice, peace, harmony and even honesty, all of which are ingredients of honest citizenship? I began to wonder. Aside from joy and intellectual fulfillment, solving mathematical problems is, by extension, an exercise for solving nonmathematical problems. Even the most complex of life's struggles can be broken into a series of simpler ones. Solving either type is one of the most rewarding journeys one can embark upon. I have dealt with my disability as a nonmathematical problem using the same or similar tactics/strategies/approaches that I utilized and valued while solving mathematical problems. Developing a plan of action is a good example of considering different options to solve a problem. While others will not have the same situation in life as I have had, the toolset is just as valuable for solving their personal challenges.

With Professor Colin Hannaford (right), Arab Thought Forum, Amman, Jordan, 2010

Professor Colin Hannaford (left) and) and Director of the Arab Thought Forum Professor Humam Ghasib (center), Amman, Jordan, 2010

We live in a world that is constantly developing. Dealing with constant change can be one of the most difficult challenges that both individuals and societies around the globe must face. Mathematical reasoning is the most innocuous facilitator of ideas, guiding change to be constructive. I would like to emphasize that the power of formal logic stands as the backbone of mathematical reasoning.

Change is undoubtedly inevitable in a world that is heavily shaped by all sorts of advancements in the sciences and technologies. While change alone may not be an option, we have a choice to make that change constructive.

In conclusion, mathematics can be seen — in the ways it's being taught and learned — as a philosophy of liberation and as a habit of mind necessary for willful and constructive adaptation.

My Teaching Philosophy

As a person who was exposed to a long history of religious, ideological, and cultural beliefs, I maintain that much of our knowledge — including our beliefs and attitudes toward mathematics — is strongly related to our history and distinct ways of living. Differences among people, including their ability to do mathematics, ought to be celebrated and appreciated.

I have lived most of my life in an electric wheelchair and have spent over three decades in the classroom with students of various mathematics backgrounds and diverse cultural legacies. I have devoted my entire adult life to helping students overcome their anxieties about mathematics. I am persuaded that with appropriate methods of teaching, with the appropriate utilization of technology, and with a deep understanding of the student's point of view, an enhancement of positive attitudes is bound to occur. Development of the student's point of view includes (1) students' perspectives about mathematics as a subject and (2) students' self-image as learners and doers of mathematics. All students can do mathematics, but this belief does not stand alone.

Students come to the mathematics classroom bringing not just their calculators but a spectrum of abilities, ideas, experiences, stories, apprehensions, and sometimes difficult conditions involving their personal lives. Many of them feel that they were deprived of necessary education and were ignored by educational institutions. Many feel lonely in their search to achieve success. Sometimes they even lack the support of their closest friends and family members. I have always striven to make a difference in my students' academic lives, their journeys in discovering the beauty of mathematics, their inner selves, and thereby discovering their own uniqueness and that of others.

By growing with my students, I have been able to share with them my own stories, struggles, dreams, and journey to this great nation. I have told them that my confinement to a wheelchair is just one difference between myself and others, a difference I celebrate and do not regret; a condition that I have lived through and do not lament; a fact that I have accepted and learned from every day of my life.

I have told my students about my love for mathematics, the rigors of mathematics, and the joy of doing mathematics. I have told them about my friends, my family, and my journey to the United States of America, all of which aided in achieving my dream of obtaining a higher education. I have told them that my dream is to remain with them in the classroom and to help them achieve their goals of becoming excellent professionals in their chosen fields of study. I have listened to my students and have encouraged them to believe that combining effort with perseverance is the only way to succeed in mathematics and throughout life. It is learning and adapting that will set them free in this global world.

Let us as teachers lead by example and help our students discover themselves as unique people with unique perspectives and identities. I believe in the power of respect, the power of mathematics, the power of words, and the power of mind and articulation. I also cherish and celebrate differences among people while encouraging genuine and credible debates in and outside the classroom.

In summary, I am calling for the continued insight into understanding citizenship, democracy, and civility through the teaching and learning of mathematics. Let us help each other develop mathematical literacy at higher levels to strengthen our appreciation and strive toward a functioning democratic society. Mathematics as a discipline has undoubtedly contributed to my own personal freedom at both the professional and intellectual levels. I hope that it will contribute to the lives of others in meaningful ways as well.

The Future of Citizenship Education

Citizenship Education through mathematics and science, as they relate to the future of culture and democracy in the United States and internationally, has been at the core of recent debates in education (Democracy and Education Journal). As a professional facing a world of economic, political, and social doubts, I began to formulate a few critical questions that require immediate attention stemming from my interest in honest citizenship. Among those questions are:

1. How can people develop a genuine understanding of citizenship through the critical and discursive exploration of mathematics and other sciences?

2. What is the formative responsibility of education in helping communities to develop perspectives to encourage the rejuvenation of our traditions which recognize the importance of mathematical and scientific proficiency?

3. What do democratic societies risk when the roles of evidence, dialogue, and intellectual leadership vanish from the spheres of public debate and popular culture? How can mathematics and the scientific method help us develop a genuine understanding of constructive democratic thinking and informed citizenship?

Education is not in complete ruin, but it is becoming desperate for a more meaningful revision. Education must enable a culture in which democratic values and ideals are not only created, but also preserved and promoted. Informed engagement in civic and political life are essential prerequisites for democracy. Democracy desperately needs education, including mathematics education.

How can that happen?

First: Through engagement and dialogue.

The implications of teaching through dialogue, like the basics of democracy, are grounded in the building of confidence and the desire to learn the unknown and to challenge all biases. One of the most interesting features of mathematics is its ethical neutrality, but the ethical principles that produce both society and mathematics can be conveyed in mathematics teaching. Dialogue encourages students to reason rather than to appeal to their teacher's authority. It allows members of a classroom the opportunity to know one another as members of a community of truth-seekers, commanding their own journeys in life. Dialogue, therefore, is essential to both education and citizenship, allowing individuals to search for the underlying hypotheses and assumptions that contribute to the shaping of one's own understanding of both the subject matter and society.

Critical thinking forms when we allow ourselves to understand the other side of the argument — entering other worlds or the worlds of others with courage, hope, wisdom, and the willingness to understand them with respect and independent pursuit. It is through excursion that thinking becomes critical, and, yes, "the excursion" can be painful as we deal with cognitive dissonance. Should we persevere, the excursion may lead us to discovery, agreement, dissent, and nowadays even sadness. Critical thinking may lead us to experience mixed emotions; it is after all the melody of the mind, and it can be seen as a measure of how free we truly are in a world of constraints, differences, and compounding anxieties.

Second: Through a willful and self-constructed understanding of change.

As mentioned earlier, change is an individual as well as a cultural phenomenon; for change to be constructive, however, it must be accompanied by moderation qualities, inside and outside the classroom, to encourage honest and genuine debates. Students at all levels unavoidably play a significant role in the shaping of their society, its institutions, and its future. These debates require students to hone their skills of critical and reflective thinking, both of which are essential for the empowerment of the individual and the advancement of knowledge.

Third: Having the courage to turn away from the student-teacher relationship and the paradox of pedagogy to examine other types of teaching and learning. All of us wrestle with this.

The function of teaching should focus on aspects related to independent thinking, intellectual inquiry, making good sense of dialogue, and giving serious consideration to students' voices.

Donald L. Finkel (2000) asked, "How can such a mutually dependent relationship between teacher and student produce independence and autonomous learning?" In *Teaching with Your Mouth Shut*, Finkel proposed an alternative vision of teaching — one that is deeply democratic in its implications. The answer involves the teacher transferring authority to the students so that they have a say in their scholastic journey while the teacher remains a source of guidance and knowledge.

Mathematics, Disability, and Problem Solving: Chapter Concluding Remarks

Throughout my life, I have experienced and confronted my disability with knowledge and skills that have enabled me to confront trials resulting from my physical impairment. This is precisely why I have developed an affinity for mathematics as a field of study. In my mind, the field of mathematics creates a mirror-image of what happens when we embark on life's journeys to find solutions to all sorts of problems, mathematical or otherwise. Those journeys demand of us a unique set of skills such as self-discipline, strategizing, pondering, flexibility, risk-taking, and analysis, all of which are employed when we aim to move forward with our thought processes.

Governed by the rules of logic and rational thinking, mathematics has provided me with an alternative to the irrational aspect of my existence, the irrational thoughts and feelings that have governed much of my life in both Palestine and the USA at different stages.

Instead of continuing to bemoan "why me?", I have allowed myself a reasonable chance and a path full of possibilities to move from "my darkness" into "our light." After all, we are all in it together, those who are able-bodied and those with special needs resulting from some physical or other impediments. It is when two or more worlds come together in a unique bond of mutual respect and genuine dialogue that a better future for all can be forged.

Luckily, science and technology evolved as models of mathematical genius during my life and have provided me with the tools I urgently needed to function independently and as a productive member of society. The evolution of mathematics turned into a revolution of the mind. In my grueling battle between body and mind, I have found refuge for myself against all odds.

In my role as a university professor, I have always aspired to demonstrate to my students the beauty of a discipline that has the promise of not only transforming entire societies and cultures, but also of altering the individual human perspective on matters of profound importance. If it's 'not me', then it's someone else who happened to be me! Mathematics is inherently honest, and it begs for questions and the most reasonable answers every step on the way toward a mathematical solution. Similarly, and if we are honest with ourselves and others, why shouldn't we be able to reach reasonable responses to our own critical and most pressing interrogations of our lives?

Chapter Six: Visiting with the Past

Introduction

Choosing the title 'Visiting with the Past' stems from a journey I took to Jordan and Palestine during the month of October 2018. However, it took me thirty-five years to return to my birthplace, the city of Nablus. I had not been back to Palestine since I left in 1983. In one sense, I was living in exile, but in another sense, I was living as a citizen with full rights and responsibilities in my newly adopted homeland, the United States of America.

Since 1993, the West Bank and the Gaza Strip were supposed to have become a state for the Palestinian people according to negotiated agreements between the Israelis and Palestinians under the auspices of the United States, the United Nations, Russia, and the European Union. The Oslo Accords signed in 1993 and in 1995 between the Palestine Liberation Organization (PLO) and Israel were never implemented, rendering hopeless the aspirations of the Palestinian people for having their own state in 22% of historic Palestine. The Accords turned out to be an arrangement to manage the conflict between the occupier and the privileged among the occupied. Managing the conflict, rather than solving it, will most likely be the strategic choice that a Zionist Israel will continue to make moving forward.

It's worthwhile to note that in 1994, Jordan and Israel signed a unilateral peace treaty ending the state of war between the two countries. Egypt and Jordan became the first two Arab countries to have full diplomatic relations with Israel. Egypt signed the Camp David Accords with Israel in 1978 under the auspices of US President Jimmy Carter.

The Palestinians, because of the Oslo Accords, came under the rule of an administrative Palestinian National Authority, but without any territorial integrity or national independence. Israel, on the other hand, continued its grip over borders and resources, only to expand its settlement activities in much of the occupied West Bank and East Jerusalem.

Settlement expansion was done contrary to the spirit of the signed agreements and international law. Elon (1997) detailed how the Palestinian-Israeli dispute was driven not so much by ancient animosity as by a series of missed opportunities, the last of which was the Oslo Accords. Fearing the establishment of a Palestinian state, Israel's right-wing policies toward the Palestinians continued to escalate before, during, and after the signing of the accords, but the assassination of Israeli Prime Minister Yitzhak Rabin by Jewish extremism in 1995 was a turning point in Israeli politics. Rabin's assassination paved the way for the election of Benjamin Netanyahu as Prime Minister of Israel in 1996. Netanyahu was known for his utter refusal for establishing not even a demilitarized Palestinian state within the 1967 borders, citing Jewish sovereignty over the occupied territories. The election of Neftali Bennett as the new Israeli Prime Minister in June of 2021 did not change Israeli attitudes toward Palestinian statehood or building more Israeli settlements in the West Bank and East Jerusalem. As a result, Israel today remains a state without a written constitution or defined borders.

The demographic character of the occupied territories has changed dramatically since I left the region in 1983.

There are an estimated 622,670 settlers in the West Bank. This figure is derived from two sources: According to data provided by Israel's Central Bureau of Statistics (CBS), at the end of 2017 413,400 people were living in the settlements of the West Bank, excluding East Jerusalem. According to data provided by the Jerusalem Institute for Israel Studies, the population of the Israeli neighborhoods in East Jerusalem numbered 209,270 people at the end of 2016.

According to the Central Bureau of Statistics, the annual growth rate of the settler population (excluding East Jerusalem) in 2017 was 1.75

times greater than that of the population in Israel: an annual increase of 3.5% in the settlements versus 2% in Israel. Approximately 60% of the increase in the settler population is accounted for by relocation [of] Israelis and the arrival of new immigrants to Israel who chose to live in settlements. (B'Tselem, 2019)

The Oslo Accords divided the West Bank into three administrative divisions: A, B and C. The distinct areas were given a different status, according to the amount of self-government the Palestinians would have over it, until a final status accord would be established. Until today, the final status negotiations have never been reached.

Areas A and B were chosen in such a way as to contain only Palestinians, by drawing lines around Palestinian population centers at the time the agreement was signed. Area C was defined as "areas of the West Bank outside Areas A and B," which, except for the issues that were to be negotiated in the permanent status negotiations, would be gradually transferred to Palestinian jurisdiction. Area A comprised approximately 18% of the West Bank; Area B about 22%. Together Areas A and B are home to about 3 million Palestinians. Area C was approximately 60% of the West Bank in which most of the settlement building intensified after signing the Oslo Accords (Area C (West Bank) 2019).

The Journey of Return

On September 29, 2018, I left Atlanta for Amman, via London. I was accompanied by a physical aid named Carlos to assist me on my journey. We arrived at Amman in the early morning on the 30th. This was my third visit to Jordan since I left Palestine in 1983. My dad used to reiterate that Nablus and Amman were his favorite cities ever. I had an affinity and love for Amman and Jordan as well. I am a proud citizen of both the United States of America and Jordan. Consequently, I lost my legal residency in Palestine (residency in the occupied territories was defined by an Israeli-issued ID card granted to Palestinians

Chapter Six: Visiting with the Past   121

following the 1967 war) after more than 30 years of an uninterrupted absence.

We arrived at the Bellevue Hotel in Amman at 2:00 a.m. The hotel is located at the second Circle. Amman is known to have eight roundabouts or circles acting as the backbone connecting the city East to West. The second Circle is famous for its location near the city center or downtown where most cultural and popular activities take place.

I spent the first three days visiting with my friends, old and new. I had a few classmates that moved to Amman from Nablus I had not seen in 35 years though we were able to reconnect through social media. I was happy and joyous to see them again so many years later.

I have always enjoyed visiting Jordan and its historical monuments. It is the home of the baptismal site of Jesus Christ, Mount Nebo, Petra, Jerash, the royal tombs, Ahl Al Kahf, the Temple of Hercules, and the Cave of the Seven Sleepers, among so many other sites. Jordan's cultural landscape combines the ancient with the innovative and the modern.

Jordan's strategic impact on the region has become central to the stability of the entire Middle East. Jordan is a close ally of the United States and the Western world in general and has played key political, economic, and financial roles in the development and politics of the whole region. It became a haven for Palestinian, Iraqi, and Syrian refugees over the last seven decades and during multiple wars that have erupted in the Middle East. Jordan is not a wealthy country with natural resources, but its human capital and education system remain one of the most advanced in the region.

In 2010, I was accompanied by my colleague Colin Hannaford from England to speak at the Arab Thought Forum led by Prince Hassan of Jordan, the brother of the late King Hussein. Prince Hassan created this forum to deal with an array of challenges confronting Arab societies and its various political systems. I was nominated during that visit to become a member of that forum. I accepted and remained a member until 2017. In 2011, the forum met in Algiers, Algeria when I had the privilege of meeting some of the most informed minds in the Arab world. In 2017, I realized that my physical condition was declining and frequent traveling to the region was not feasible.

Historic Roman city of Tipaza, Algiers, 2011

Traveling to Jordan and Algeria revealed the massive area in which the Roman Empire was created. The architectural nature of the Roman ruins I witnessed as a child in Sebastia, a Roman site, now a Palestinian village near my birth city Nablus, and then later what I saw in Jerash, Jordan, and Tipaza, Algeria, was breathtaking and mind-boggling. I could not help but wonder how an empire with such massive power, geography, autonomy, and influence had crumbled and ceased to exist!

In 2013, I went to Jordan along with 10 Mercer University students as part of a university program known as 'Mercer on Mission'. I was accompanied by my adopted son Sami, who for the very first time was able to travel outside of the United States at the age of 16.

On that expedition to Jordan, I was also accompanied by my dear friend Professor Duane Davis and his wife Mary. Duane had been enjoying his retirement since 2008, but I was able to talk him out of retirement for the duration of that summer.

The Mercer on Mission program requires Mercer students to enroll in two academic courses and commit to a service-learning project while abroad. I taught one of the two courses on topics related to the political, cultural, and historical landscape of the Middle East, while Duane taught a course on the religion of Islam. Duane's academic background in philosophy and religion made him the best fit for such a course, and what an incredible experience it was for all of us involved in such a project.

For the duration of three weeks, we were privileged to work at an educational and recreational summer camp with children from SOS Children's Village Association of Jordan, a local, private, nonpolitical, nongovernmental, and independent social development organization. The program, through its academic component, assessed the current debates in the Arab world: relation of Islam to politics; civil society in the Middle East; status of women and minorities. Included in that assessment were the explanations of cultural institutions and social processes related to the behavior of individuals, their needs, values, and motivations. The program also explained the Middle East as a distinct cultural area by focusing on generalized problems, patterns, and cultural processes. Mercer students were able to describe the area in terms of major topics of ethnicity, kinship, religion, leadership, patterns of living, sex roles, and family life.

> SOS Children's Villages Jordan is a national non-profit organization established in 1983, by her Majesty Queen Noor Al-Hussein who is the Honorary President. The Association cares for over 30% of orphaned and vulnerable children in Jordan […] in 32 houses, 3 villages and 9 youth houses in the cities of Amman, Irbid and Aqaba.
>
> The SOS Children's Villages concept is based on four main pillars: a mother, brothers and sisters, a home, and a village. An SOS mother

cares for 5 to 7 children in a house that replicates the setting of a family. (SOS Children's Villages Jordan 2021)

The day camp was held five days a week for two weeks at the Al-Asriyya Schools campus in Amman. The children arrived each morning by bus at 9:30 and returned to the village where they live at 2:30 in the afternoon. The Mercer students directed the children in various indoor and outdoor activities, including singing, dancing, building, and painting model houses, table games, sports, artwork, English language instruction, and storytelling.

SOS Children's Village Association of Jordan Summer Camp
Mercer on Mission, Amman, Jordan, 2013

Visiting My Birthplace after 35 Years

On this 2018 trip to Jordan, Carlos and I were exploring historical sites, visiting the local markets, and anxiously preparing for crossing the Jordan River into the West Bank for my first visit to Nablus and Palestine in 35 years.

Chapter Six: Visiting with the Past   125

On October 6, 2018, I gave a lecture at the American University of Madaba on the relationship between democratic thinking and mathematics. The next day, Carlos and I headed down to the Jordan Valley preparing to cross the border into the West Bank, a border that is fully controlled by the Israeli government.

President Nabil Ayyoub (my left) and faculty members from the American University of Madaba, Jordan, 2018

While in Amman, I was able to use wheelchair accessible transportation that I arranged prior to my departure from the USA. The drive to the Jordan Valley took us from an elevation of nearly 2500 feet above sea level to about 1400 feet below sea level near the Dead Sea. The border crossing was at the Allenby Bridge, also known as the King Hussein Bridge, connecting mainly the West Bank, but also Israel, to Jordan.

When we arrived at the Israeli-controlled border, we checked our luggage, passed through security, and then were granted a three-month visa. The Israeli security at the border crossing treated me with absolute respect. At some point, I was asked to be seated in a regular chair to inspect my manual wheelchair, but when I explained that I was unable to stand up, the security officer with the approval of a supervisor wished me good luck on my trip.

En route to the Jordan Valley, anticipating re-entry to Palestine

Although I normally use an electric wheelchair, on this trip to the West Bank I chose to use a manual wheelchair. I made that choice to avoid any delays at the border crossing, given that a manual wheelchair would be much easier to inspect from a security standpoint. The second reason, far more compelling, was that I could not find any car rentals for a wheelchair-accessible transportation in Nablus. They simply did not exist.

Not being able to rely on wheelchair-accessible transportation during my visit, I had to rely on a manual Hoyer lift (a lift specifically designed for transferring individuals unable to stand up from one seat to another) that I could use to get into a regular car.

Prior to my departure, I experimented with the lift to verify its functionality: being able to get in and out of a regular car. The experiment was a total success.

I was thrilled finally to know that I could use a regular car for transportation purposes. Carlos, my assistant and caregiver on this trip, was able to use it with ease. It took three minutes to get in, or out of, any car.

Mixed Emotions and Tears

After clearing Israeli customs at the border, we entered a nearby Palestinian welcoming area controlled by a Palestinian police force near Jericho. After exiting from that area, I was greeted by Suleiman, a friend from Nablus, who was waiting at the exit gate. I was finally able to make it back to my homeland. I did it against all odds thirty-five years later. It was around 5:00 p.m., October 7th, a date that was engraved in my soul and my memory! All I cared about at that moment was reaching my city of birth, Nablus, even on a tourist Visa! Adrenaline was rushing throughout my body.

A sea of emotions erupted as we embarked upon a short visit to the historical city of Jericho nearby. I was trying to remember places I visited as a child or as a teenager, but very little seemed to match what was left in my memory. So many things seemed to have changed: agriculture, architecture, transportation, and highways. People's moods reflected skepticism and cynicism about their political future.

We left Jericho and began the drive up the mountains and hills from the Jordan Valley leading to Nablus in the northern part of the West Bank. We were traveling in areas B and C of the West Bank. The orange sunset behind the hills and mountains was breathtaking.

Despite the passing of thirty-five years, some features have remained the same, while others were impossible to recognize. The conflict between Palestinians and Israelis was ongoing, evidenced by the ever-increasing number of Jewish settlements in the West Bank and East Jerusalem. The presence of Israeli soldiers was evident near every settlement in the Jordan Valley and was visible all the way to the entrance of the city of Nablus. Once we entered the city borders in area A, a Palestinian police force assumed responsibility for security and public safety.

Feelings of exuberance and sadness began to flood my soul. The saga of the Oslo peace accords was apparently nothing but an arrangement, mostly for security purposes. The evidence of peace that many had envisioned between Israelis and Palestinians because of those accords was nowhere to be found.

On the outskirts of the city of Nablus, as we approached its eastern entrance from the nearby town of Howara and the Balata refugee camp, there was a sign informing travelers that they were about to enter Area A, which was under the Palestinian Authority administrative rule. Area A, as I have outlined before, housed the major Palestinian cities with the highest density of inhabitants. It has its own Palestinian police force, but the Israeli army could enter it at any time for whatever reason it deemed necessary, especially for security purposes. Israeli forces would coordinate with Palestinian security prior to the entry, but at times this protocol was not followed. Although meaningful negotiations reached a dead end, security cooperation between the Israeli government and the Palestinian Authority remained intact.

My mind and soul turned into a sea of thoughts and mixed emotions on the way to Nablus. I could not help but think about my memories, my life, the Palestinian people I left behind, and their aspirations to live in freedom. The West Bank, mainly in Areas B and C, throughout the so-called Oslo peace process had been swallowed by blocks of newly built Jewish-only settlements. Those blocks of settlements had a network of roads connecting them; they had their own electricity and water supplies. Although some roads and highways were shared by Israelis and Palestinians in areas B and C, Jewish settlements across the West Bank and East Jerusalem were, for the most part, connected by a network of roads and highways built for the sole use of Jewish settlers.

The West Bank was no longer a contiguous geographic area. It was broken into small scattered noncontiguous geographic territories not viable for the establishment of a Palestinian state. The dream of having a two-state solution to the Israeli-Palestinian conflict seemed to have been a missed opportunity of historical proportions.

Chapter Six: Visiting with the Past

I will not get into the details of what specifically caused the collapse of the Oslo Accords, but I will quickly highlight the two main reasons: extreme hardline policies of successive Israeli governments, and a divided Palestinian society.

The idea of an independent Palestinian state was frightening to Israeli claims of sovereignty stemming out of religious and ideological perspectives. The future of East Jerusalem as the capital of an independent Palestinian state was damaging to Israeli claims that Jerusalem was the eternal and the undivided capital of the Jewish state. Building more Jewish settlements in the occupied territories was seen by successive Israeli governments as an Israeli right based on their interpretations, deep convictions, and popular support. Exercising Israeli sovereignty and control over the occupied territories did not take into consideration international law, UN resolutions, or the spirit of the signed agreements with the Palestinian Authority.

The Palestinians, on the other hand, were discouraged by continuing Israeli settlement activities on their land, rendering it impossible for them to have a viable and a contiguous state. Palestinians living in Gaza chose the Islamic Hamas movement to lead them, while those living in the West Bank remained under the rule of the Palestinian Authority. Unlike the Palestinian Authority, Hamas does not believe in Israel's right to exist as an independent state and sees it as an extreme expression of western colonialism.

On October the 8th, I was scheduled to meet with the President of Al-Najah National University, Dr. Maher Natsheh, during which we talked about supportive programs available for students with disabilities on campus as they pursue their higher education. We also talked about higher education in Palestine and the challenges being faced under the Israeli occupation and the future aspirations of the Palestinian people.

In honor of my life journey, Al-Najah National University presented to me its Prestige Plate of Distinction decorated with the University's image, October 2018

I was extremely impressed by the university's infrastructure on both of its campuses, old and new. The university is the largest Palestinian university with a population of over 22,000 students. The distance between the two campuses was no more than 1 km or little more than a half-mile.

On October 9th I took a trip to the old city of Jerusalem. Although I had visited Jerusalem numerous times during my childhood, I never had the chance to visit the Old City given its terrain and very old infrastructure that was not handicap friendly by any modern standards. On this trip, I was determined with the help of Carlos to spend the entire day in the alleys and neighborhoods of the Old City.

Chapter Six: Visiting with the Past 131

In front of Bab Al-Amoud (Damascus Gate), one of 12 gates to the Old City of Jerusalem, October 2018

In front of the Dome of the Rock, Jerusalem, October 2018

In front of the entry to the Church of the Holy Sepulcher, Jerusalem, October 2018

The Wailing Wall (Alburaq Wall for Muslims), Jerusalem, October, 2018

On October the 10th, I met with university students with disabilities, their families, and community members to talk about my journey as a person with a physical disability. Students with visual, hearing, and physical impairments along with their families and friends were present during my presentation. Following the presentation was a session devoted to questions and answers about all sorts of aspects related to disability: accessibility, laws, identity, personhood, technologies, cultural attitudes, and belief systems. I left the presentation impressed with the resiliency and determination of those students. In all, there were 146 students with disabilities, mostly visual, enrolled at the university during that academic year.

With a group of students with disability, October 2018

After my presentation, I was invited to eat lunch with one of my old classmates and the director of the Office of Students with Disabilities on campus, an office that caters to the needs of all 146 students.

It was clear to me that substantial progress has been made regarding the plight of people with disabilities. For the first time, I was able to see users of electric wheelchairs roaming the streets of the city. Advocacy groups and laws pertaining to the rights of people with disabilities were established. For the most part, the campus was accessible to students with physical challenges allowing them to enroll and participate in an academic setting. Public awareness and ongoing social conversations surrounding the lives of people with disabilities provided me with renewed hope and optimism about the future of

Palestinian society. However, advanced assistive technologies and wheelchair-accessible public transportation were nowhere to be seen.

This new and evolving reality brought back memories of my departure in 1983 and the complete lack of accessibility and the overall dismal climate surrounding attitudes toward people with disabilities. However, on this journey I was encouraged with what I had been able to witness.

On October 11th, I gave a public presentation at the Nablus Municipality Public Library sponsored by the non-governmental organization (NGO) "Seeds for Development and Culture". Following my talk, I was awarded the City Plaque of Nablus by the Mayor of the city.

I spent October 12th touring the city with an old friend one last time. I was preparing myself to say my second farewell to my birth city and all those I was about to leave behind. "Will I ever be able to see you again, my beloved Nablus?" I asked repeatedly!

Early morning, October 13th at 6:00 a.m., Suleiman's aunt, Ghada, arrived at the Al Yasmeen Hotel with the taxi driver who drove me and Carlos to the Jordan Valley. We were ready to cross the border heading back to Jordan. After a one-day rest in Amman, we flew back to the US on October 15th.

I am indebted to Ms. Ghada Amad for her tireless logistical efforts in making my return visit to Palestine a dream come true.

Chapter Six: Visiting with the Past   135

Mayor of Nablus, Mr. Adly Yaish and Nablus municipal council member
Ms. Samah Al-Kharouf, October 2018

City Plaque of Nablus

An outdoor public gathering in honor of my life journey at the Nablus Municipality Public Library, one of the oldest libraries in Palestine

Sunrise over the Jordan Valley on the way back to Jordan during the early hours of October 13, 2018

Reflections on a Six-Day Visit

During my short visit to Palestine, I could not help but remember the phrase by the late Dr. Martin Luther King, Jr. who said, "We must discover the world over, and we must learn to live together as brothers or we will all perish together as fools" (Oumar, 2015).

I have been absent from this place for nearly four decades and the political reality has not changed. The scenery and the people have changed, but the suffering of the Palestinian people continues.

I began to ponder the new and ongoing reality of the conflict. There were many more Israeli settlements in the West Bank. There was a visible lack of full autonomy and independence for the Palestinians. I was horrified by learning more about the Israeli blockade since 2007 and how it turned the Gaza Strip into a massive prison.

I also witnessed the devastating reality of a divided Palestinian society. Palestinians living in the West Bank were ruled by the Palestinian Authority, which was dominated and controlled by the secular Fatah movement, while Palestinians living in the Gaza Strip were ruled by the religious group Hamas. The lives of Palestinians living in the Gaza Strip, before and after the Oslo Accords, were loaded with misery, desperation, and suffering (Hass, 2000)[5].

During this visit and for the very first time, I was able to witness the Israeli West Bank barrier, a separation wall 442 miles long of which 85% was built by Israel on Palestinian lands to separate Israelis and Palestinians from one another, akin to the old Berlin Wall. Of the 442 miles, nearly 300 miles have been completed (United Nations, 2021).

---

[5] Amira Hass was nominated for the Robert F. Kennedy Award for her book Drinking the Sea at Gaza: Days and Nights in a Land Under Siege. The misery intensified during and after several Israeli wars on Gaza.

Israel claimed that the wall was built by the Israeli government to create a 'safer' Israel. However, as the wall was being built, new Israeli settlements and settlement blocks were launched in the occupied territories. The strategy was to establish an 'on the ground reality' making it impossible for any future negotiations to succeed and never to revert to the status quo ante. Israel has never missed a single pretext in its entire history to build more and more of its illegal settlements in lands it occupied. Building settlements is at the heart of political and religious Zionism. Unfortunately, building more settlements in the West Bank and East Jerusalem took place with tacit approval from the US Government. In public, several US administrations have been critical of Israeli decisions to build more settlements, but the reality on the ground was speaking differently.

To fully understand why there is no peace before and after the signing of the Oslo Accords, one must read the book *Deliberate Deceptions* by Paul Findley (1995), late member of the US House of Representatives from Illinois. In his book, Findley, who served in the House for 22 years, dispels the myths and outlines the facts about the US-Israeli relationship. This relationship is basically dominated and controlled by the powerful Israeli lobby, a Judeo-Christian evangelical alliance, and US interests in the Middle East. There are common and key strategic interests between Israel and the United States. Such interests include access to natural resources (oil), maintaining geopolitical influence in the region, and always guaranteeing Israel's security and military superiority.

Everything I witnessed during my visit was pointing at an endless struggle between two peoples locked in conflict instead of common humanity. Palestinian grievances, however, remain morally, ethically, and logically sound! The Zionist narrative has been challenged worldwide by the ongoing practice of ethnic cleansing of Palestinians by systemic and calculated Israeli policies (Pappe, 2015).

During my visit I wondered about those selfish decisions that were made by the British government a century ago when Palestine was under a British mandate. Did England, under the rule of its High Commissioner in Palestine, Herbert Samuel, have the moral, legal, or political rights to facilitate the transfer of Palestine to another people, the Jewish People, after the signing of the Belfour Declaration in 1917?

The answer is obviously 'no', but the shocking reality before my own eyes was extremely overwhelming.

As I was traveling in the West Bank and Jerusalem, I could not help but think about those egotistically calculated policies of the British government during that time under the influence of Zionist beliefs (Rodinson, 1973).

It is worthwhile mentioning here that more than 100 new laws were established under the leadership of Samuel allowing the transfer of Palestinian lands into Zionist hands (MissSunriseNorth, 2013 21:42). These laws were adopted to facilitate Jewish immigration to Palestine.

The Palestinians, far more than ever before, are determined today to achieve their national independence in 22% of historic Palestine despite the call by many of them to establish it in all of historic Palestine.

Israel in 1948 was introduced as a colonial project (Khalidi et al., 1992); Pappe, 2015; Rodinson, 1973). Today, the challenges for Israel are greater than ever before. Israeli society has been moving to the far right in terms of its politics and its refusal to implement the Oslo Accords by continuing to build more settlements. The policies of ethnic cleansing that began in 1948[6] by expelling nearly 700,000 Palestinians (half the population) and depopulating at least 418 Palestinian villages beg the question: "What's next?"

---

[6] The reader is strongly encouraged to watch the documentary, 1948 Creation & Catastrophe (2019) detailing the events leading to the creation of the State of Israel and Palestinian Nakba (Catastrophe).

The colonial project that began in 1948 continues today and will likely continue indefinitely unless the ambitions of Zionism, religious and political, come to a halt.

US President Donald Trump, during his term in office, complicated matters far more than anyone could have expected. His administration disregarded international law and UN resolutions by extending and recognizing Israeli sovereignty over East Jerusalem and the Golan Heights, making peace between the involved parties much more difficult to attain. Instead of advancing peace and justice between the involved parties in the conflict, President Trump advanced unilateral peace treaties between Israel and key Arab states such as the United Arab Emirates and Morocco, as well as Sudan and Bahrain. By doing so, he gave the impression that he was a peacemaker. Those countries, however, were outside the parameter of an actual conflict with Israel. Legitimizing Israel among Arab states, already divided and weak, was at the forefront of US foreign policy during the Trump administration. The key issue in the Middle East today remains to be the plight of the Palestinian people and the suffering they have endured for so long. Any diversion from the real issue would only complicate matters and extend the status quo for decades to come.

Driving the Palestinians out of their homeland by Israeli policies and practices after 1948 has failed. There is today an equal number of Palestinians and Israeli Jews living between the Mediterranean Sea and the Jordan River, approximately 13 million in total.

Giving up has never been — and will never be — an option for the Palestinian people, as it was not an option for me throughout my journey as a Palestinian American.

My return to Palestine 35 years later has brought to my attention the following grim realities:

1- The Palestinian Authority has failed the aspirations of the Palestinian people in terms of establishing an independent state in the West Bank and the Gaza Strip, with East Jerusalem as its capital, after a quarter of a century of direct and indirect negotiations with Israel. According to a special report that was published in the Middle East Monitor (Ramah, 2013), the spread of corruption is "endemic within the Palestinian Authority and society" and has made it much more difficult for the Palestinians to achieve any type of real and strong presence at the negotiation table. The Palestinian Authority was allowed to play the role of a security officer as it has colluded with the Israeli government against its own people. VIP treatments were extended to Palestinian key officials by Israel as a gratitude for their security cooperation.

2- In addition to being an occupying power, Israel has turned into an apartheid system of government. Israel has constantly been trying to reconcile the irreconcilable. On one hand it wants to be a nation state of the Jewish people under the 'Basic Law' adopted in 2018, and on the other hand it wants to be a democratic state. The language of this law secured the Jewishness of the state in the minds of Israeli Jews. The explicit language in the Declaration of Independence in 1948, which spoke of Israel as a Jewish and democratic state with equality among all its citizens, was nowhere to be found in the Basic Law, rendering it exclusive of non-Jews. According to Avnery, "the Israeli Supreme Court adopted the principles of the Declaration without a legal basis. The Basic Law, however, was a binding Israeli law" (*Who the hell are we?* 2018).

The fact that 20% of Israeli citizens are Palestinians and the fact that there are approximately 6.5 million Palestinians living in Israel or under Israel's military occupation may not be easy to comprehend. There is an equal number of Jews living in the same area. This fact makes it impossible to reconcile the national identity of the state with its claims of being democratic. The right of return is not even granted to Palestinians who were expelled in 1948, contrary to UN resolution 194. However, any

Jew in the world under the Israeli 'Law of Return' passed in 1950 can immigrate to Israel anytime and claim Israeli citizenship immediately.

3- The massive spread of Israeli settlements, with nearly 630,000 Jewish settlers in the West Bank and East Jerusalem, is impossible to reverse. If Israeli settlements in the occupied territories are an expression of Israeli sovereignty, then there is no hope for the establishment of a Palestinian state.

4- Therefore, the two-state solution is impossible to implement unless fundamental shifts in Israeli policies and directions take place among policymakers and on the ground. This reality alone provides for sufficient cause to contemplate the idea of creating a binational state for both Israelis and Palestinians.

Justice according to international law and human rights organizations is not an experimental design! It is not rooted in trials. Admittance of wrongdoing is a prerequisite for peace with justice. Healing, if there is ever to be peace between Israelis and Palestinians, will undoubtedly take a very long time.

The Palestinians are under occupation and have no choice than to resist just as the Americans resisted against Britain before their own independence and the Native Americans before their own assimilation or destruction. There is a fundamental clash of ideas and aspirations among Israelis and Palestinians. Ultimately, Israel must make a choice: either continue to exist as an example of apartheid and colonial practices and policies (Yazan, 2021) or as a state that abides by international law. Israel has no choice but to reexamine its own identity, but this is unlikely given the political forces and coalitions within Israeli society and ruling governments.

Chapter Seven: Conclusion

My story would have been much different had I stayed in Palestine, but I am thankful for my journey and my new country, the United States of America. It is in America that I became free.

In this book, I wanted to share my personal journey to inspire as many people as I could to reach their goals and aspirations. My chances of living a full life in Palestine would have been slim. I know there is nothing like home, but home is also where your possibilities and dreams unfold.

It pains me to see the people of Palestine continue to suffer under Israeli occupation and the rule of an authoritarian and corrupt Palestinian Authority. It hurts to see the foolishness of a world that seeks genuine peace without justice, hope without dreams, and freedom without responsibility. My new home is the United States of America with its incredible Constitution, institutions, founding values and principles, and its secular and democratic political system.

I hope the United States will carry out its foreign policy in the Middle East, especially toward the Palestinian people, justly and evenhandedly and as an honest broker. This is unlikely, given the historic and enormous power held by the Israeli lobby and Christian Zionists (Ball, George W. & Douglas B, 1992).

I am convinced that any future peace between Israelis and Palestinians, if there is ever one to be found, requires the work and goodwill of all parties — Arabs and Jews, Palestinians and Israelis, and the whole international community. Neither religion nor political extremism can provide viable solutions to the existing conflict. International law is the only means to achieve peace with justice.

My opportunities arose because of the goodwill of people from all walks of life. I have crossed many personal and professional bridges with success. My dreams came true with the help of countless others.

It is my hope that peace with justice will prevail as the people in the Middle East and the whole world continue their search for a better life with renewed promises. It is through education and a community comprised of seekers of goodwill and empathy that we will be able to reach a better understanding of what unites us all — common humanity. When indifference prevails, we are all at risk.

Courage and honesty can make the ultimate difference in the outcomes we seek as we live. Unfortunately, all paths in life involve a level of suffering. Suffering is tragic, and while all but inescapable, the lessons learned from suffering must teach us empathy toward others as it helps us find our own strengths within. To live in peace with others and ourselves, the images of a universe that has been violated and shattered either by tragedy or misfortune must be confronted. The ultimate lesson is never to inflict suffering purposefully upon ourselves or others. This is the only way to prevent indifference from prevailing.

Giving up should not be our option. Despite my disability, I will continue to implement my dream to live to the fullest until the very end. Giving up has never been, and will never be, my option.

With courage, honesty, and empowerment by countless others, I was empowered to confront my universe of misfortune with an innate power of endurance and persistence, as an affirmation of what is possible. Fortunately, and throughout my life, I have learned that education, courage, and risk-taking are necessary elements in the search for realistic alternatives. It has been said, "Strangers in a new culture see only what they know." If true, then defying oddity commands us to contemplate what is possible.

Finally, no people should relinquish their rights to freedom and liberty under democratic rule. The world should not stray from the path of democracy and justice for all. Let us not forget, however, that democracy is a fragile concept as it constantly demands the attention of an informed citizenry. We must not give up or slow down our pursuit for a peaceful and just world. Complacency in the face of injustice is not an option.

References

Adiv, A., & Schwartz, M. (1992). *Sharon's star wars: Israel's seven Star settlement plan.* Hanitzotz A-Sharara.

Area C (West Bank). (2019, September 13). In Wikipedia. https://en.wikipedia.org/w/index.php?title=Area_C_%28West_Bank%29&oldid=915532259.

Beit-Hallahmi, B. (1993). *Original sins reflections on the history Of Zionism and Israel.* Olive Branch Press, an imprint of Interlink Publishing Group, Inc.

Benvenisti, M. (2002, January 18). Systematically Burying Ourselves. *Ha'Aretz.*

Bogdan, R. C., & Biklen, S. K. (2007). *Qualitative Research for Education: An introduction to theory and methods.* Allyn and Bacon. (Original work published in 1982)

B'Tselem, The Israeli Information Center for Human Rights in the Occupied Territories. (n.d.). *About B'Tselem.* About B'Tselem. Retrieved September 13, 2019, from https://www.btselem.org/about_btselem.

B'Tselem, The Israeli Information Center for Human Rights in the Occupied Territories. (2019, January 16). *Statistics on settlements and settler population.* Statistics on Settlements and Settler Population. Retrieved September 13, 2019, from https://www.btselem.org/settlements/statistics.

Carter, J (2006). *Palestine: Peace not apartheid.* Simon and Schuster.

Cheshin, A., Hutman, B., & Melamed, A. (2002). *Separate and unequal the inside story of Israeli rule in East Jerusalem.* Harvard University Press.

Deir Yassin remembered. Deir Yassin Remembered. (2018, July 28). *Retrieved August 19, 2020, from* https://www.deiryassin.org/.

Elon, A. (1997). *A blood-dimmed tide: Dispatches from the Middle East.* Columbia University Press.

Ezrahi, Y. (1999). *Rubber bullets: Power and conscience in modern Israel.* Farrar Straus & Giroux.

Findley, P. (1995). *Deliberate deceptions: Facing the facts about the u.s.-israeli relationship.* Lawrence Hill Books.

Finkel, D. L. (2000). *Teaching with your mouth shut*. Boynton/Cook Publishers.

Finkelstein, N. G. (2015). *The Holocaust industry: Reflections on the exploitation of Jewish suffering*. Verso.

Hass, A. (2000). *Drinking the sea at Gaza: Days and nights in a land under siege*. Henry Holt.

Hixson, W. L. (2021). In *Architects of repression: How Israel and its lobby put racism, violence and injustice at the center of US Middle East Policy* (p. 15). essay, Institute for Research: Middle Eastern Policy, Inc.

Hurwitz, D., & Meyer, M. T. (1992). In *Walking the red line: Israelis in search of Justice for Palestine* (p. 16). introduction, New Society Publishers.

Jewish Voice for Peace. Facebook. (n.d.). Retrieved October 19, 2020, from https://www.facebook.com/Jewish-Voice-for-Peace-186525784991/.

Khalidi, W., Elmusa, S., & Khālidī Muḥammad 'Alī. (1992). *All that remains: The Palestinian villages occupied and depopulated by Israel in 1948*. Institute for Palestine Studies.

Lee, K. P. (2010). *A guide to writing mathematics*. University of California, Davis.

Mellin-Olsen, S. (2002). *The politics of mathematics education*. Kluwer Academic.

MissSunriseNorth. (2013, July 13). Al-Nakba ~ Part 01. YouTube. https://www.youtube.com/watch?v=qCgHwkEprVo.

Morris, B. (2001). *Righteous victims: A history of The Zionist-Arab Conflict, 1881-1999*. Vintage Books.

Nablus. (2020, June 13). In Wikipedia. https://en.wikipedia.org/w/index.php?title=Nablus&oldid=961268124.

New York State Independent Living Council, Inc. (2018). *Michael Peluso (posthumous)*. Home. Retrieved November 17, 2019, from https://nysilc.org/inductees/28-2018/151-michael-peluso.

Oumar, S. (2015, April 25). *Live together as brothers or PERISH together as FOOLS Dr Martin Luther King Jr.* YouTube. https://www.youtube.com/watch?v=TuvEijvTXuw.

Palestinian Academic Society for the Study of International Affairs - Jerusalem. (n.d.). *TUQAN, QADRI.* PASSIA. http://www.passia.org/personalities/815.

Pappe, I. (2015). *The ethnic cleansing of Palestine.* Oneworld.

Ramah, S. (2013, December). Corruption in the Palestinian Authority. https://www.aman-palestine.org/cached_uploads/download/migrated-files/itemfiles/b2a7e241322895ba53fdd6425a55c40a.pdf.

Rodinson, M. (1973). *Israel: A Colonial-settler state?* Monad Press; distributed by Pathfinder Press.

Roy, S. (2019, September). *The Impossible Union Of Arab And Jew: Reflections On Dissent, Remembrance And Redemption. 2008 EDWARD SAID MEMORIAL LECTURE.* Adelaide, Australia; The University of Adelaide.

Ruhl, C. (2020, August 9). *William James biography and contributions to psychology.* William James | Simply Psychology. https://www.simplypsychology.org/william-james.html#:~:text=William%20James%20Biography%20and%20Contributions%20to%20Psychology,-By%20Charlotte%20Ruhl&text=James'%20two%20main%20schools%20of,idea%20can%20never%20be%20proven.

Said, E. W. (2004). *Orientalism.* Vintage Books.

SOS Children's Villages Jordan. SOS Jordan. (n.d.). https://sos-jordan.org/en/who-we-are/sos-childrens-villages-jordan/.

Spinal muscular atrophy (sma) - diseases. Muscular Dystrophy Association. (2021, April 29). https://www.mda.org/disease/spinal-muscular-atrophy.

Syracuse, New York. (2021, October 8). https://en.wikipedia.org/w/index.php?title=Syracuse%2C_New_York&oldid=1048904066.

Tivnan, E. (1987). *The Lobby: Jewish political power and American foreign policy.* Simon and Schuster.

United Nations. (2021, May 17). *In facts and figures - question of Palestine*. United Nations. Retrieved June 12, 2021, from https://www.un.org/unispal/in-facts-and-figures/.

Wesleyan University. (n.d.). Middle Eastern Studies. Retrieved April 22, 2021, from https://www.wesleyan.edu/mes/arabic/index.html.

Who the hell are we? Uri Avnery | Uri's Column | since 1993. (2018, August 4). Retrieved November 18, 2021, from http://uriavnery.com/en/hatur.html.

Yazan. (2021, June 24). *A threshold crossed*. Human Rights Watch. Retrieved November 12, 2021, from https://www.hrw.org/report/2021/04/27/threshold-crossed/israeli-authorities-and-crimes-apartheid-and-persecution.

Zochrot. (2014). *'Arab al-Nufay'at*. Zochrot. Retrieved November 13, 2019, from https://www.zochrot.org/en/village/49313.

Zochrot. (2014). *Our vision.* Zochrot - Our Vision. Retrieved November 13, 2019, from

https://www.zochrot.org/en/content/17.

Lightning Source LLC
Chambersburg PA
CBHW051619010526
44119CB00008B/201